# THE LUNCHBOX BOOK

# THE LUNCHBOX BOOK

## EMMA-LEE GOW & JANET SMITH

**EBURY PRESS**
LONDON

Published by Ebury Press
Division of The National Magazine Company Ltd
Colquhoun House
27–37 Broadwick Street
London WIV IFR

First impression 1988

ISBN 0 85223 765 0

Editor Barbara Croxford
Designer Grub Street Design
Illustrator Tony Hannaford
Photographer Paul Moon
Stylist Maria Jacques
Cookery Maxine Clarke

Filmset by Advanced Filmsetters (Glasgow) Ltd
Printed and bound in Singapore by Imago Publishing

**Published with the assistance of the
National Peanut Council of America.**

# CONTENTS

# INTRODUCTION

 A lunchbox should be healthy, tasty and fun. In dietary terms, it should contain about a third of your child's daily nutritional requirements. In this book, with the help of twenty-three colour photographs, we show you how to balance a lunchbox to achieve these aims. At the back we have also included a selection of interchangeable soups, breads, pitta and sandwich fillings, cakes and biscuits to help you to devise your own combinations.

Baking your own breads, cakes and biscuits may seem unnecessary, but in doing so you ensure that they are low in salt, sugar and fat and contain no artificial additives and, most important of all, they'll be tasty too!

We have given a rough guide to portion size, but this is only an estimate. Simply increase or decrease the quantities according to your child's age and appetite. Always try to include a portion of salad or a piece of fresh fruit, even if your child is not too keen. Include the occasional home-made sweet treat in preference to the shop-bought variety. All the baking recipes give quantities for a batch, so you can store or freeze the remainder for a later date.

## INGREDIENTS

We suggest you keep the following items in your storecupboard or refrigerator ready to make up a healthy lunchbox at a moment's notice.

**American peanuts or peanut butter** Weight for weight, peanuts contain more protein than beef, chicken or fish. Peanuts are useful for adding crunch to salads, cakes and breads; while peanut butter is indispensable as a sandwich spread, alone or with honey, fruit or jam, or as a dressing, mixed with mayonnaise or yogurt.

•

**Natural yogurt** Useful for making dressings or for mixing with fresh fruit for a quick dessert.

•

**Low fat soft cheese** The ideal sandwich or cake filling, flavoured with honey, nuts or herbs. It can also be thinned down to make dressings.

•

**Mayonnaise** Try to use the low fat version. Use alone or mix with natural yogurt or lemon juice and flavour with herbs, tomato purée, curry paste or mustard to make an infinite number of salad dressings and sandwich 'moisteners'.

•

**Oranges, lemons and limes** Useful for making freshly squeezed juice-based drinks or for flavouring dressings, cakes and biscuits; all keep well in the refrigerator.

**Rice and pasta shapes** Useful for quick, filling salads or to add bulk and fibre to soups and stews.

•

**Dried beans** Make nutritious pâtés, dips, spreads or salads. Useful for adding protein to soups and stews.

•

**Canned beans** Same as above, but quicker! Choose the sugar-free varieties.

•

**Canned tomatoes** Good as the basis of soups and stews.

•

**Canned fish** Mackerel, tuna, sardines and salmon all make quick, tasty sandwich fillings or pâtés. Choose those canned in brine.

•

**Dried fruits** Dried apricots, dates, prunes, peaches and pears all make good sweet treats in a lunchbox. They can also be chopped or puréed for inclusion in salads, cakes or breads.

•

**Wholemeal and white flour, sugar, polyunsaturated margarine, easy blend yeast, poppy seeds, sesame seeds, chocolate, cocoa powder, rolled oats, vegetable oils** All these ensure that you can 'make up' a wide range of breads, cakes and pastries.

•

**Honey/syrup/treacle** Good for flavouring yogurt, soft cheese or as a sweetener.

**Home-made or reduced sugar jams** Ideal fillings for cakes or sandwich biscuits as well as for spreading on chunks of home-made bread or scones.

•

**Tomato purée/mild mustard/soy sauce** All useful for flavouring salad dressings.

## PACKING A LUNCHBOX

There is no need to go to great expense buying specially manufactured containers. Yogurt, salad and soft cheese pots and cartons can all be washed and reused for transporting salads, dips and jellies. Cover with plastic wrap if they don't have lids. Most foods can be transported in one of these small lidded containers or wrapped in plastic wrap, greaseproof paper, foil, a napkin or a plastic bag. Drinks can be transported in lidded beakers or vacuum flasks. Soups and stews should be carried in wide-necked vacuum flasks.

## STORAGE

Make up batches of rolls, breads, cakes, biscuits and buns, then wrap and freeze. Simply thaw the amount required each day. Likewise, soups and stews can be frozen in individual portion size and then thawed as required.

Made-up salads, sandwich fillings and spreads are best stored in the refrigerator. We indicate the storage time at the end of each recipe.

# FARMYARD

## TUNA AND MAYONNAISE TOASTS

• Serves 2 •

polyunsaturated margarine, for spreading
4 slices of wholemeal bread, crusts removed
105 g (3½ oz) can tuna fish in brine, well
   drained and flaked
2 spring onions, trimmed and chopped
30 ml (2 tbsp) mayonnaise
30 ml (2 tbsp) natural yogurt
salt and pepper

**1** Spread the margarine on one side of each
bread slice.

**2** Combine the tuna, onions, mayonnaise and
yogurt together in a bowl. Season to taste with
salt and pepper.

**3** Divide the filling between 2 slices of bread.
Cover with the remaining slices of bread,
margarine side down. Toast each side under a
hot grill for 1–2 minutes. If liked, large biscuit
cutters can be used to cut out a large shape
from the sandwich when toasted. Cool.

**Packing and storage** Wrap in greaseproof paper
for transporting. Best eaten on the day of making.

## TINY TOMATO SALAD

• Serves 2 •

15 ml (1 tbsp) sesame seeds
225 g (8 oz) cherry tomatoes, halved
3 basil leaves, roughly chopped
15 ml (1 tbsp) olive oil
5 ml (1 tsp) vinegar
1.25 ml (¼ tsp) runny honey
salt and pepper

**1** Toast the sesame seeds in a dry frying pan
until golden brown. Combine the tomatoes,
basil and sesame seeds in a bowl.

**2** Whisk together the oil, vinegar, honey and
season to taste with salt and pepper. Pour over
the tomatoes and toss all the ingredients
lightly. Chill in the refrigerator until ready for
transporting.

**Packing and storage** Spoon into small lidded
containers for transporting. Store in the refrigerator
for up to 2 days.

## ANIMAL BISCUITS

• Makes about 15 •

50 g (2 oz) polyunsaturated margarine
50 g (2 oz) soft light brown sugar
1 egg yolk
50 g (2 oz) plain wholemeal flour
75 g (3 oz) plain white flour
finely grated rind and juice of ½ lemon
50 g (2 oz) icing sugar, sifted

**1** Lightly grease a baking sheet. Beat the
margarine and sugar together in a bowl until
pale and creamy. Beat the egg yolk in.

**2** Fold in the flours with the lemon rind and
juice and mix to a smooth dough. Wrap the
dough and chill for 20 minutes.

**3** Roll out the dough on a lightly floured
surface to 0.5 cm (¼ inch) thickness. Using an
animal shape cutter, cut out the desired shapes.
Bake at 190°C (375°F) mark 5 for 10–15
minutes. Transfer to a wire rack and leave to
cool.

**4** Put the icing sugar into a small bowl.
Gradually stir in 7.5 ml (1½ tsp) warm water.
The icing should be thick enough to coat the
back of the spoon thickly.

**5** Put the icing into a small piping bag fitted
with a fine nozzle or make a paper icing bag,
cutting the tip off to make a very fine hole.
Carefully pipe squiggly lines across the animals
or make decorative markings. Leave to set.

**Packing and storage** Wrap in plastic wrap or greaseproof paper for transporting. Store in an airtight container for up to 1 week.

# WARM MALTED MILK

• Serves 2 •

*30 ml (2 level tbsp) malted drink powder*
*568 ml (1 pint) milk*

**1** In a jug, mix the malted drink powder with 30 ml (2 tbsp) hot water to make a smooth paste.

**2** Bring the milk to the boil in a saucepan and gradually pour on to the blended powder, stirring all the time.

**Packing and storage** Pour into vacuum flasks for transporting. Make and drink on the same day. Shake well before drinking.

9

# TRAIN

## RIBBON LAYERED SANDWICHES

• Serves 4 •

polyunsaturated margarine, for spreading
6 slices of bread, crusts removed
90 ml (6 tbsp) mayonnaise
30 ml (2 tbsp) natural yogurt
salt and pepper
100 g (4 oz) can salmon, drained and flaked
30 ml (2 tbsp) chopped fresh parsley
100 g (4 oz) cooked chicken, chopped
10 ml (2 tsp) tomato purée

1 Spread the margarine on one side of each slice of bread.

2 Mix the mayonnaise and yogurt together in a bowl. Season to taste with salt and pepper.

3 Put the salmon and parsley in a bowl and beat together with half of the mayonnaise dressing.

4 Purée the chicken, tomato purée and remaining dressing in a blender or food processor until smooth.

5 On one slice, spread half of the salmon filling. Place the second slice on top and spread with the remaining filling. Place the third slice, margarine side down, on top. Repeat with the remaining bread and chicken filling.

6 Wrap the layered sandwich in greaseproof paper and store in the refrigerator until ready for transporting. Slice each layered sandwich loaf into 1 cm (½ inch) thick slices and cut each slice crossways in half.

**Packing and storage** Wrap in greaseproof paper for transporting. Store in the refrigerator for up to 1 day.

## STUFFED DATES

• Serves 4 •

12 fresh dates
100 g (4 oz) full fat soft cheese, low fat cheese or cottage cheese, sieved
50 g (2 oz) walnuts, roughly chopped
chopped walnuts, to garnish

1 Using the point of a small knife, slit open the dates on one side and carefully remove the stones without spoiling the shape of the dates.

2 Beat the cheese and walnuts together in a bowl. Using a teaspoon, fill the dates with the cheese mixture. Sprinkle with chopped walnuts and arrange in small paper cases.

**Packing and storage** Wrap in plastic wrap or foil for transporting. Store in the refrigerator for up to 1–2 days.

## TWO-TONE GRAPE JUICE

• Serves 4 •

450 ml (¾ pint) unsweetened white grape juice
450 ml (¾ pint) unsweetened red grape juice

1 Mix together the white and red grape juice in a jug. Chill in the refrigerator until ready for transporting.

**Packing and storage** Pour into lidded beakers for transporting. Store in the refrigerator for up to 1 week.

# MINI-FRUIT CHEESECAKES

• Makes 12 •

**For the pastry**
75 g (3 oz) plain wholemeal flour
75 g (3 oz) plain white flour
10 ml (2 level tsp) soft light brown sugar
pinch of salt
75 g (3 oz) polyunsaturated margarine

**For the filling**
100 g (4 oz) full fat soft cheese, curd cheese or
  cottage cheese, sieved
1 egg
25 g (1 oz) soft light brown sugar
finely grated rind and juice of ½ small lemon
Greek strained yogurt and fresh fruit, to
  decorate

1  Lightly grease twelve patty tins. To make the pastry, put the flours, sugar and salt in a bowl. Rub in the margarine until the mixture resembles fine breadcrumbs. Add enough water to bind the ingredients and mix to form a smooth dough.

2  Thinly roll out the dough on a lightly floured surface. Cut out twelve rounds using a fluted cutter and use to line the prepared tins. Line with foil or greaseproof paper and baking beans.

3  Bake 'blind' at 200°C (400°F) mark 6 for 10 minutes. Remove the foil or greaseproof paper and baking beans, then return to the oven for a further 5 minutes until lightly browned.

4  Meanwhile, to make the filling, put the cheese, egg, sugar, lemon rind and juice in a bowl and beat until smooth. Pour the filling into the pastry cases.

5  Lower the oven temperature to 150°C (300°F) mark 2 and bake the cheesecakes for 15 minutes or until the fillings are set. Transfer to a wire rack and leave to cool. When completely cool, chill in the refrigerator until ready for transporting. When required, decorate the top of each cheesecake with yogurt and fresh fruit.

**Packing and storage**  Wrap in plastic wrap or greaseproof paper for transporting. Store in an airtight container for up to 2–3 days, or wrap and freeze.

# SPACEMAN

## HALF MOON PASTIES

• Serves 4 •

**For the pastry**
100 g (4 oz) plain white flour
100 g (4 oz) plain wholemeal flour
large pinch of salt
100 g (4 oz) polyunsaturated margarine

**For the filling**
15 ml (1 tbsp) olive oil
1 small onion, skinned and chopped
1 garlic clove, skinned and crushed
225 g (8 oz) lean minced beef
200 g (7 oz) can tomatoes, chopped
1 large carrot, scrubbed and diced
pinch of dried oregano
salt and pepper
1 egg yolk, to glaze

1 To make the pastry, put the flours and salt
into a bowl. Rub in the margarine until the
mixture resembles fine breadcrumbs. Add
enough water to bind the ingredients together
and mix to form a smooth dough. Set aside
while making the filling.

2 To make the filling, heat the oil in a saucepan
and fry the onion and garlic until just soft. Add
the minced beef, tomatoes, carrot and oregano.
Season to taste with salt and pepper and
simmer for 15–20 minutes, stirring frequently.
Leave to cool.

3 Roll out the dough on a lightly floured
surface and cut out 4 12.5 cm (5 inch) rounds.
Divide the mince filling between the rounds.
Brush the edges with egg yolk and fold in half to
make a semi-circle. Press the edges together to
seal. Re-roll any trimmings, cut out small
initials and place on top of pasties to decorate.

4 Brush the pasties with egg yolk and place on
a baking sheet. Bake at 200°C (400°F) mark 6 for
30–40 minutes or until golden and crisp.
Transfer to a wire rack and leave to cool. Serve
with lettuce, if liked.

**Packing and storage** Wrap in greaseproof paper,
paper napkin, plastic wrap or foil for transporting.
Store in the refrigerator for up to 3 days, or wrap and
freeze.

# STARRY SOUP

• Serves 4 •

2 large potatoes, peeled and chopped
1 large leek, trimmed and finely chopped
2 large carrots, scrubbed and finely chopped
2 celery sticks, trimmed and finely chopped
1.1 litres (2 pints) hot vegetable stock
15 ml (1 tbsp) tomato purée
50 g (2 oz) small dried star-shaped pasta
salt and pepper
2 slices of bread, crusts removed
15–30 ml (1–2 tbsp) vegetable oil

1  Put half of the potatoes, leek, carrots and celery in a large saucepan with the stock and tomato purée and bring to the boil. Cover and simmer for about 25 minutes.

2  Cool slightly, then purée the soup in a blender or food processor until smooth. Return to the pan. Add the remaining chopped vegetables. Simmer for 10 minutes, then add the pasta stars and cook for a further 10–15 minutes or until the pasta and vegetables are tender. Season to taste with salt and pepper.

3  To make the croûtons, cut the bread into star shapes using a small cutter. Heat the oil in a frying pan and fry the bread stars until golden and crisp, turning frequently. Drain the croûtons on absorbent kitchen paper. Serve the soup hot with the croûtons.

**Packing and storage**  Pour into vacuum flasks for transporting. Wrap the croûtons separately. Store in the refrigerator for up to 1 week, or pour into a lidded container and freeze.

# SATURN SURPRISE

• Serves 4 •

300 ml ($\frac{1}{2}$ pint) Greek strained yogurt
2 red plums, halved and stoned
225 g (8 oz) blackcurrants, thawed if frozen
300 ml ($\frac{1}{2}$ pint) red grape juice
10 ml (2 tsp) runny honey
15 g ($\frac{1}{2}$ oz) powdered gelatine
Greek strained yogurt and blackcurrants, to decorate

1  Cover the base of 4 individual containers with 150 ml ($\frac{1}{4}$ pint) of the yogurt. Top each with a plum half, stoned side down.

2  Put the blackcurrants, grape juice and honey in a saucepan and simmer gently for 5–10 minutes until softened.

3  Purée the blackcurrant mixture in a blender or food processor until smooth. Sieve into a bowl and set aside.

4  Put 60 ml (4 tbsp) water in a small heatproof bowl and sprinkle in the gelatine. Stand the bowl in a saucepan of hot water and stir over the heat for 2–3 minutes or until the gelatine has dissolved.

5  Beat the gelatine into the blackcurrant purée. Carefully fold in the remaining yogurt. Spoon around the plum, so that the top of the plum is still showing. Swirl with a little yogurt and blackcurrants, to decorate. Chill overnight.

**Packing and storage**  Cover the containers with a lid or plastic wrap for transporting. Store in the refrigerator for up to 1–2 days.

# MOON ROCK BISCUITS

• Makes about 12–16 •

50 g (2 oz) polyunsaturated margarine
75 g (3 oz) soft light brown sugar
50 g (2 oz) plain chocolate, melted
1 egg
few drops of vanilla flavouring
50 g (2 oz) self-raising white flour
50 g (2 oz) self-raising wholemeal flour
pinch of salt
50 g (2 oz) chocolate chips
50 g (2 oz) walnuts, chopped
icing sugar, for dusting

1  Grease 2 baking sheets. Cream the margarine with the sugar and chocolate in a bowl until light and fluffy. Beat in the egg and vanilla flavouring. Add the remaining ingredients and stir thoroughly.

2  Drop heaped teaspoonfuls of the mixture on to the prepared baking sheets. Bake at 180°C (350°F) mark 4 for 12–15 minutes or until firm to the touch. Cool on the baking sheets for a few minutes, then transfer to a wire rack and leave to cool. Dust lightly with sifted icing sugar.

**Packing and storage**  Wrap in plastic wrap or foil for transporting. Store in an airtight container for up to 1 week, or wrap and freeze.

# HALLOWE'EN

## COLESLAW

• Serves 4 •

450 g (1 lb) hard white cabbage
1 red eating apple
15 ml (1 tbsp) lemon juice
2 carrots, scrubbed and coarsely grated
2 celery sticks, trimmed and sliced
½ green pepper, seeded and cut into thin strips
45 ml (3 tbsp) chopped fresh parsley
25 g (1 oz) sultanas
60 ml (4 tbsp) mayonnaise
60 ml (4 tbsp) natural yogurt
salt and pepper

1 Remove the core and any discoloured leaves from the cabbage. Shred very finely. Quarter, core and thinly slice the apple and toss in the lemon juice.

2 In a large bowl, combine the vegetables and apple together with the parsley and sultanas.

3 Mix the mayonnaise and yogurt together and season to taste with salt and pepper. Pour over the vegetables and toss until well coated.

**Packing and storage** Spoon into small lidded containers for transporting. Store in the refrigerator for up to 2–3 days.

## PIZZA FACE

• Serves 4 •

2 wholemeal muffins
225 g (8 oz) can mackerel fillets in tomato sauce
50 g (2 oz) hard cheese, finely grated

**For the face**
2 black olives, stoned and each cut into 4 slices
4 thin strips of green pepper

1 Cut the muffins in half. Mash the mackerel fillets and spread evenly over each muffin half.

2 Sprinkle the cheese on the top half of each muffin to represent hair. Cook under a hot grill until the cheese has browned.

3 Decorate each muffin half with the slices of olives for the eyes and pepper for the mouth. Cool completely before wrapping.

**Packing and storage** Wrap in greaseproof paper or plastic wrap for transporting. Best eaten on the day of making.

## HONEYCOMB APPLE JELLIES

• Serves 4 •

300 ml (½ pint) milk
2 eggs, separated
25 g (1 oz) soft light brown sugar
15 g (½ oz) powdered gelatine
300 ml (½ pint) apple juice

1 Put the milk in a heavy-based saucepan and heat until hot, but not boiling. Beat the egg yolks with the sugar in a bowl until thick and creamy. Pour in the warmed milk, whisking all the time. Strain back into the saucepan and stir until thick.

2 Put 60 ml (4 tbsp) water in a small heatproof bowl and sprinkle in the gelatine. Stand the bowl in a saucepan of hot water and stir over the heat for 2–3 minutes or until the gelatine has dissolved.

3 Beat the gelatine and apple juice into the custard and set aside until the mixture starts to thicken.

4 Whisk the egg whites until stiff but not dry and fold into the custard mixture. Pour into 4 individual containers or jelly moulds and chill overnight. Serve with fresh fruit, if liked.

**Packing and storage** Cover the containers with a lid or plastic wrap for transporting. Store in the refrigerator for up to 1–2 days.

## ORANGE DREAM DRINK

• Serves 4 •

*3 oranges*
*about 600 ml (1 pint) pineapple juice*
*natural yogurt and strips of orange rind, to*
  *decorate*

**1** Finely grate the rind from the oranges and place in a jug. Squeeze the juice from the oranges and add to the jug.

**2** Make up the juice to 750 ml (1¼ pints) with pineapple juice and stir well. Chill in the refrigerator until ready for transporting.

**Packing and storage** Pour into lidded beakers for transporting. Top with a large swirl of yogurt and a few orange rind strips. Store in the refrigerator for up to 2 days.

15

# COUNTRY PICNIC

## ORCHARD SALAD

• Serves 4 •

**For the salad**
450 g (1 lb) red cabbage
1 large ripe pear
15 ml (1 tbsp) lemon juice
4 rashers of crispy cooked bacon, chopped
100 g (4 oz) hard cheese, grated
50 g (2 oz) walnuts, roughly chopped
4 spring onions, trimmed and sliced

**For the dressing**
90 ml (6 tbsp) vegetable oil
30 ml (2 tbsp) pear juice
2.5 ml ($\frac{1}{2}$ tsp) runny honey
salt and pepper

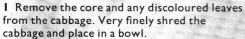

**1** Remove the core and any discoloured leaves from the cabbage. Very finely shred the cabbage and place in a bowl.

**2** Quarter, core and thickly slice the pear and toss in the lemon juice, then add to the bowl with the remaining salad ingredients.

**3** To make the dressing, place the oil, pear juice and honey in a small bowl and whisk together. Season to taste with salt and pepper. Pour over the salad and toss together lightly.

**Packing and storage** Pack into lidded containers for transporting. Store in the refrigerator for up to 2 days.

6

# Hedgehog Rolls

• Makes 8 •

225 g (8 oz) strong wholemeal flour
225 g (8 oz) strong white flour
large pinch of salt
50 g (2 oz) polyunsaturated margarine
1 sachet of easy blend yeast
beaten egg yolk, to glaze
16 sultanas

1  Grease a baking sheet. Put the flours and salt into a bowl and rub in the margarine. Add the yeast and mix well. Add about 300 ml (½ pint) tepid water to give a fairly soft dough.

2  Turn out the dough on to a lightly floured surface and knead for about 10 minutes until elastic and no longer sticky. Divide the dough into 8 pieces. Shape each piece into an oval-shaped roll and press one end into a point to represent a 'nose'. Place on the prepared baking sheet and cover with a clean tea-towel. Leave in a warm place for about 30 minutes or until doubled in size.

3  Brush the rolls all over with beaten egg yolk. Using the points of kitchen scissors, snip each roll to create 'spikes', leaving the nose end plain. Arrange 2 sultanas to represent the eyes.

4  Bake at 230°C (450°F) mark 8 for 15–20 minutes or until golden brown. Transfer to a wire rack and leave to cool.

**Packing and storage** Split and spread with a little polyunsaturated margarine, then wrap in plastic wrap or greaseproof paper for transporting. Store in an airtight container for up to 1–2 days, or wrap and freeze.

# Jolly Jam Tarts

• Makes 12 •

75 g (3 oz) plain wholemeal flour
75 g (3 oz) plain white flour
10 ml (2 level tsp) soft light brown sugar
pinch of salt
75 g (3 oz) polyunsaturated margarine
reduced sugar jam, to fill

1  Lightly grease twelve patty tins. Put the flours, sugar and salt in a bowl. Rub in the margarine until the mixture resembles fine breadcrumbs. Add enough water to bind the ingredients and mix to form a smooth dough.

2  Thinly roll out the dough on a lightly floured surface. Cut out twelve rounds using a 7.5 cm (3 inch) fluted cutter and use to line the prepared tins. Fill each pastry case one-third full with jam. Re-roll any trimmings and cut out small shapes. Place one on top of each tart to decorate.

3  Bake at 200°C (400°F) mark 6 for 10–15 minutes or until the pastry is lightly browned. Transfer to a wire rack and leave to cool.

**Packing and storage** Wrap in plastic wrap or paper napkins for transporting. Store in an airtight container for up to 1 week.

# Harvest Yogurt Drink

• Serves 4 •

2 large ripe pears, peeled, cored and chopped
15 ml (1 tbsp) lemon juice
150 ml (¼ pint) natural yogurt
300 ml (½ pint) unsweetened apple juice
30 ml (2 tbsp) runny honey

1  Purée all the ingredients in a blender or food processor until smooth. Chill in the refrigerator until ready for transporting.

**Packing and storage** Pour into lidded beakers or vacuum flasks. Store in the refrigerator for up to 1–2 days.

# SAILING

## Puffy Chicken Pie

• Makes 12 •

2 chicken breast fillets, skinned
30 ml (2 level tbsp) plain flour
15 ml (1 tbsp) vegetable oil
100 g (4 oz) button mushrooms, sliced
150 ml ($\frac{1}{4}$ pint) milk
50 g (2 oz) frozen peas
salt and pepper
212 g (7$\frac{1}{2}$ oz) packet puff pastry
beaten egg, to glaze
sesame seeds, for sprinkling

1 Grease a baking sheet. Cut the chicken into small pieces and toss in the flour. Heat the oil in a pan and gently fry the chicken and mushrooms until the chicken changes colour.

2 Gradually stir in the milk and bring to the boil, stirring all the time. Stir in the peas and season to taste with salt and pepper. Cover and simmer gently for 5–10 minutes. Cool.

3 Roll out the pastry on a lightly floured surface to a 30.5 cm (12 inch) square. Cut into twelve squares. Divide the chicken mixture between the pastry squares. Brush the edges with a little of the beaten egg, then fold each diagonally in half. Crimp the edges together to seal.

4 Place the pies on the prepared baking sheet and brush with the remaining beaten egg. Sprinkle with sesame seeds. Bake at 220°C (425°F) mark 7 for 15–20 minutes or until golden brown. Leave to cool.

**Packing and storage** Wrap in foil or plastic wrap for transporting. Store in the refrigerator for up to 2–3 days, or wrap and freeze.

## Pineapple Salad

• Serves 4 •

150 g (5 oz) can pineapple rings in natural juice, drained with juice reserved
75–100 g (3–4 oz) beansprouts
3 carrots, scrubbed and cut into matchstick strips
15 ml (1 tbsp) vegetable oil
few toasted cashew nuts, roughly chopped

1 Cut pineapple into small chunks. Mix with the beansprouts and carrots.

2 Mix 60 ml (4 tbsp) of the reserved juice with the oil and pour over the salad just before transporting. Sprinkle with the cashew nuts.

**Packing and storage** Spoon into small lidded containers for transporting. Store in the refrigerator for up to 1–2 days.

## Jelly Wobble

• Serves 4 •

600 ml (1 pint) orange, apple, grape or mango juice
1 envelope powdered gelatine
fresh fruit in season (not kiwi fruit or pineapple), cut into small pieces

1 Put 300 ml ($\frac{1}{2}$ pint) of the fruit juice in a saucepan and sprinkle over the gelatine. Heat very gently until the gelatine has dissolved. Do not boil. Add the remaining fruit juice.

2 Pour half the liquid into 4 individual jelly moulds or small plastic containers and arrange the fresh fruit on top. Leave in the refrigerator to set.

3 Pour on the remaining jelly and chill until set.

**Packing and storage** Cover with lids or plastic wrap for transporting. Store in the refrigerator for up to 2–3 days.

# SUMMER SHAKE

• Serves 4 •

*225 g (8 oz) summer berries, such as*
*strawberries, raspberries, blackcurrants*
*900 ml (1½ pints) milk*
*honey, to taste*

**1** Purée the fruit in a blender or food processor
until smooth. Pour in the milk and honey to
taste. Mix thoroughly together. Chill in the
refrigerator until ready for transporting.

**Packing and storage** Pour into lidded beakers or
vacuum flasks for transporting. Store in the
refrigerator for up to 2–3 days.

19

# AMERICAN FOOTBALL

## CHEESY EGGS IN A CRUNCHY NEST

• Serves 4 •

700 g (1½ lb) potatoes, peeled and cut into
   chunks
salt and pepper
50 g (2 oz) Cheddar cheese, grated
30 ml (2 tbsp) chopped fresh parsley
4 hard-boiled eggs
wholemeal flour
beaten egg, for coating
100 g (4 oz) fresh wholemeal breadcrumbs

For the salad
few radishes
50 g (2 oz) alfalfa or mustard and cress
little lemon juice

1 Well grease a baking sheet. Cook the
potatoes in a saucepan of boiling salted water
for 20 minutes or until tender. Drain. Mash
with the cheese and parsley and season to taste
with salt and pepper. Cool.

2 Shell the eggs. Divide the potato mixture
into 4 portions and shape each into a round
large enough to wrap around an egg. Dust the
eggs with a little flour then wrap each in a
potato round. Press the edges together to seal.

**3** Dip in the beaten egg and then coat in breadcrumbs. Place the coated eggs on the prepared baking sheet. Cook at 200°C (400°F) mark 6 for 20–25 minutes, turning once. Leave to cool.

**4** To make the salad, thinly slice the radishes and cut each slice in half. Mix with the alfalfa or mustard and cress and a little lemon juice.

**Packing and storage** Arrange nests of salad in small lidded containers and place an egg on top of each. Store the eggs in the refrigerator for up to 1–2 days. The salad is best eaten on the day of making.

# FRUIT AND NUT BARS

• Makes 12 •

*450 g (1 lb) eating apples, peeled, cored and finely chopped*
*225 g (8 oz) mixed dried fruit such as sultanas, dates, apricots, chopped if necessary*
*100 g (4 oz) American honey roasted peanuts*
*75 g (3 oz) self-raising wholemeal flour*
*25 g (1 oz) desiccated coconut*
*90 ml (6 tbsp) apple juice*
*45 ml (3 tbsp) vegetable oil*

**1** Grease an 18 cm (7 inch) square tin. Put the apples in a heavy-based saucepan with 15 ml (1 tbsp) water. Cover tightly and cook gently until the apples are very soft. Uncover and cook, stirring all the time until all of the moisture has evaporated.

**2** Add the remaining ingredients to the apple and beat thoroughly together. Spoon into the prepared tin and level the surface.

**3** Bake at 170°C (325°F) mark 3 for 40–45 minutes or until firm to the touch and light brown. Mark into twelve bars. Leave to cool in the tin.

**Packing and storage** Wrap in greaseproof paper or plastic wrap for transporting. Store in an airtight container for up to 2 weeks.

# VITALITY DRINK

• Serves 1–2 •

*juice of 1 orange*
*juice of 2 grapefruits*
*juice of 1 large lemon*
*1 egg*
*15 ml (1 tbsp) runny honey*
*15 ml (1 level tbsp) wheatgerm*

**1** Work the fruit juices, egg, honey and wheatgerm in a blender or food processor until well mixed. Chill in the refrigerator until ready for transporting.

**Packing and storage** Pour into a lidded container for transporting. Best drunk on the day of making.

# DOLLS' PLAYTIME

## MINTY MUSHROOM SALAD

• Serves 4 •

100 g (4 oz) burghul wheat
100 g (4 oz) button mushrooms, thickly sliced
2 spring onions, trimmed and chopped
30 ml (2 tbsp) chopped fresh mint
45 ml (3 tbsp) chopped fresh parsley
finely grated rind and juice of 1 lemon
30 ml (2 tbsp) olive oil
salt and pepper

1 Put the burghul wheat in a bowl and pour over enough boiling water to cover by about 2.5 cm (1 inch). Leave to soak for 10 minutes or until all of the water is absorbed.

2 Fluff up the wheat with a fork and stir in the remaining ingredients. Mix together well. Chill in the refrigerator until ready for transporting.

**Packing and storage** Spoon into small lidded containers for transporting. Store in the refrigerator for up to 2–3 days.

## CHICKEN-ON-A-STICK WITH PEANUT SAUCE

• Serves 4 •

25 g (1 oz) creamed coconut
45 ml (3 tbsp) crunchy peanut butter
30 ml (2 tbsp) lemon juice
30 ml (2 tbsp) soy sauce
chilli powder, optional
2.5–5 ml ($\frac{1}{2}$–1 level tsp) ground coriander
2.5–5 ml ($\frac{1}{2}$–1 level tsp) ground cumin
2 chicken breast fillets, skinned
15 ml (1 tbsp) vegetable oil
1 garlic clove, skinned and crushed
cucumber chunks, to accompany

1 Put the coconut, peanut butter, 15 ml (1 tbsp) of the lemon juice and 15 ml (1 tbsp) of the soy sauce in a pan with the chilli powder, if using, the coriander, cumin and 150 ml ($\frac{1}{4}$ pint) water. Bring slowly to the boil, then simmer for a few minutes until thickened. Leave to cool.

2 Cut the chicken into small chunks and thread on to blunted wooden cocktail sticks or small bamboo skewers. Mix the oil with the remaining lemon juice, soy sauce and the garlic and pour over the chicken. Leave to marinate if you have time.

3 Cook the chicken under a hot grill for 10–15 minutes, turning frequently. Serve with the sauce for dipping and the cucumber chunks.

**Packing and storage** Pour the sauce into small pots and wrap the chicken and cucumber in foil for transporting. Store in the refrigerator for up to 1 day.

## BISCUIT FRUIT TARTS

• Serves 4 •

30–45 ml (2–3 tbsp) low fat cream cheese or
    fromage frais
honey, to taste
4 digestive biscuits
slices of fruit such as kiwi, star fruit,
    tangerines

1 Mix the cheese with a little honey to taste, then spread on to the biscuits.

2 Arrange the sliced fruit on top.

**Packing and storage** Wrap in foil or plastic wrap for transporting. Do not store.

22

# Yogurt Whizz

• Serves 4 •

300 ml (½ pint) low fat natural yogurt
15–30 ml (1–2 tbsp) honey
450 ml (¾ pint) fruit juice
1 egg white, size 6

**1** Mix all the ingredients together in a jug. Chill in the refrigerator until ready for transporting.

**Packing and storage** Pour into lidded beakers for transporting. Shake vigorously before drinking to create a foam on top of the drink. Best drunk on the day of making.

# BEACH

## CHICKEN DRUMSTICKS

• Serves 4 •

30 ml (2 tbsp) tomato purée
30 ml (2 tbsp) Worcestershire sauce
10 ml (2 tsp) runny honey
5 ml (1 tsp) Dijon mustard
4 chicken drumsticks

1 Mix the tomato purée, Worcestershire sauce, honey and mustard together. Make 2–3 deep slashes on each drumstick and brush all over with the tomato mixture.

2 Leave to marinate if time permits.

3 Cook the chicken under a hot grill, turning frequently, for 15–20 minutes or until crisp and golden and cooked through. Serve cold.

**Packing and storage** Wrap in foil for transporting. Store in the refrigerator for up to 1–2 days. Freezing not recommended.

## ORANGE RICE SALAD

• Serves 4 •

100 g (4 oz) long-grain brown rice
finely grated rind and juice of 1 orange
50 g (2 oz) sultanas
30 ml (2 tbsp) chopped fresh mint
30 ml (2 tbsp) vegetable oil

1 Cook the rice in a saucepan of boiling salted water for about 30 minutes or until just tender. Drain and rinse with boiling water.

2 Mix in the remaining ingredients. Leave to cool.

**Packing and storage** Spoon into small lidded containers for transporting. Store in the refrigerator for up to 1 week.

## DATE AND BANANA BREAD

• Makes 450 g (1 lb) teabread •

2 large ripe bananas
225 g (8 oz) self-raising wholemeal flour
10 ml (2 level tsp) ground mixed spice
100 g (4 oz) polyunsaturated margarine
100 g (4 oz) soft light brown sugar
100 g (4 oz) stoned dates, chopped
2 eggs

1 Grease and line a 450 g (1 lb) loaf tin. Peel and mash the bananas in a bowl. Beat in the remaining ingredients until well mixed.

2 Pour the mixture into the prepared tin and level the surface. Bake at 180°C (350°F) mark 4 for 50–60 minutes or until firm to the touch. Turn out on to a wire rack and leave to cool.

**Packing and storage** Slice and wrap in plastic wrap for transporting. Store in an airtight container for up to 3–4 days, or wrap and freeze.

## FRESH FRUIT YOGURT

• Serves 4 •

600 ml (1 pint) low fat natural yogurt
225 g (8 oz) fresh fruit, such as apples, bananas, pears, tangerines, strawberries or raspberries, chopped
honey, to taste

1 Mix the yogurt with the chosen fruit and honey to taste.

**Packing and storage** Spoon into small lidded containers for transporting. Best drunk on the day of making.

# PAINTBOX

## FRESH TOMATO SOUP

• Serves 4 •

15 ml (1 tbsp) vegetable oil
1 medium onion, skinned and chopped
25 ml (1½ level tbsp) plain white flour
600 ml (1 pint) chicken stock
450 g (1 lb) ripe tomatoes, skinned
30 ml (2 tbsp) tomato purée
10 ml (2 level tsp) brown sugar
salt and pepper

1  Heat the oil in a saucepan and fry the onion for 5–8 minutes until golden brown. Stir in the flour and cook for 1–2 minutes, stirring. Gradually stir in the stock, bring to the boil and simmer while preparing the tomatoes.

2  Halve the tomatoes and scoop out the seeds into a sieve. Roughly chop the flesh. Press the seeds to extract all the juice and pulp. Discard the seeds. Add to the soup with the chopped tomato flesh.

3  Add the remaining ingredients, cover and simmer gently for 20–30 minutes until mushy.

4  Cool slightly, then purée the soup in a blender or food processor. Reheat.

**Packing and storage**  Pour into vacuum flasks for transporting. Store in the refrigerator for up to 1–2 days, or pack and freeze.

## MINI CHEESE SCONES

• Makes about 24 •

100 g (4 oz) self-raising wholemeal flour
100 g (4 oz) self-raising white flour
pinch of salt
50 g (2 oz) polyunsaturated margarine
100 g (4 oz) hard cheese, finely grated
about 150 ml (¼ pint) milk

1  Grease a baking sheet. Put the flours and a pinch of salt in a bowl. Rub in the margarine until the mixture resembles fine breadcrumbs. Stir in 50 g (2 oz) of the cheese and enough milk to make a fairly stiff dough.

2  Roll out the dough on a lightly floured surface until about 2 cm (¾ inch) thick. Cut into rounds or small shapes with a cutter measuring about 4 cm (1½ inches) across. Put on the prepared baking sheet.

3  Brush the scones with milk and sprinkle with the remaining cheese. Bake at 220°C (425°F) mark 7 for about 8–10 minutes or until golden brown. Transfer to a wire rack and leave to cool.

**Packing and storage**  Split and spread with a little polyunsaturated margarine. Wrap in plastic wrap or plastic bags for transporting. Store in an airtight container for up to 1–2 days, or wrap and freeze.

## BEANY SALAD

• Serves 4 •

75 g (3 oz) French beans, halved and cooked
213 g (7 oz) can red kidney beans, drained
100 g (4 oz) ham or hard cheese, diced
1 carrot, scrubbed and thinly sliced
30–45 ml (2–3 tbsp) mayonnaise
30 ml (2 tbsp) thick natural yogurt
5 ml (1 tsp) curry paste or tomato purée

1  Mix French beans with the kidney beans, ham and carrot. Combine other ingredients and spoon over the salad.

**Packing and storage**  Spoon into small lidded containers for transporting. Store in the refrigerator for up to 1–2 days.

# Bull's Eye Biscuits

• Makes 40 •

*150 g (5 oz) plain wholemeal flour*
*150 g (5 oz) plain white flour*
*175 g (6 oz) polyunsaturated margarine*
*75 g (3 oz) caster sugar*
*15 ml (1 level tbsp) cocoa powder, sifted*
*few drops of almond essence*

**1** Lightly grease 2–3 baking sheets. Beat the flours, margarine and sugar together in a bowl to give a fairly stiff dough.

**2** Cut the dough in half. Work the cocoa powder into one half and the almond essence into the other. Cut each piece of dough in half.

**3** Roll one of the chocolate dough halves into a roll about 25.5 cm (10 inches) long. Roll out one of the almond dough halves into a sheet long enough and wide enough to encase the chocolate. Roll around the chocolate log, pressing the edges to seal.

**4** Repeat with the remaining dough, but using the almond mixture to make the roll and the chocolate mixture to encase it. Chill the rolls for 1 hour until firm.

**5** Cut the rolls into 1 cm ($\frac{1}{2}$ inch) slices and place on the prepared baking sheets. Bake at 190°C (375°F) mark 5 for 15–20 minutes. Transfer to a wire rack and leave to cool.

**Packing and storage** Place in a plastic bag for transporting. Store in an airtight container for up to 2–3 weeks, or wrap and freeze.

# Apple Juice

• Serves 2–3 •

*3 large eating apples, cored*
*rind and juice of 1 lemon*
*runny honey, to taste*
*apple slices, dipped in lemon juice, and mint leaves, to decorate*

**1** Cut the apples into thin slices crossways. Place in a large jug or bowl with the lemon rind and juice. Pour over 600 ml (1 pint) boiling water. Cover and leave to cool for several hours.

**2** Strain the apple juice. Sweeten to taste with honey. Chill in the refrigerator until ready for transporting. Float apple slices and mint leaves on top of the drink to serve.

**Packing and storage** Pour into lidded plastic beakers for transporting. Store in the refrigerator for up to 1 week.

# JIGSAW

## SPINACH SOUP

• Serves 4 •

450 g (1 lb) fresh spinach, washed and
   trimmed, or 225 g (8 oz) packet frozen
   spinach, thawed
900 ml (1½ pints) vegetable stock
1 small onion, skinned and finely chopped
few drops of tabasco sauce
pinch of grated nutmeg
salt and pepper
150 ml (¼ pint) single cream

1 Put all the ingredients, except the cream, in a
saucepan and simmer for 10–15 minutes or
until the onion is soft.

2 Cool slightly, then purée the soup in a
blender or food processor until smooth. Return
to the saucepan and reheat. Swirl in the cream.

**Packing and storage** Pour into vacuum flasks for
transporting. Store in the refrigerator for up to
1 week.

## SAVOURY BITES AND STRIPY SALAD IN PITTA POCKETS

• Serves 4 •

225 g (8 oz) chick peas, soaked overnight
1 medium onion, skinned and finely chopped
1 garlic clove, skinned and crushed
30 ml (2 tbsp) tahini
5 ml (1 level tsp) ground cumin
30 ml (2 tbsp) peanut butter
salt and pepper
100 g (4 oz) wholemeal breadcrumbs
1 egg, beaten

For the stripy salad
few radicchio or red cabbage leaves
few Cos lettuce leaves
4 small pitta breads, to serve

1  Grease a baking sheet. Drain the chick peas. Put into a saucepan, cover with plenty of water and boil for 1–1½ hours or until tender. Drain.

2  Put the chick peas into a blender or food processor with the remaining ingredients. Purée until smooth.

3  Divide the mixture into 16–18 small balls. Bake at 180°C (350°F) mark 4 for 20 minutes or until golden brown. Leave to cool.

4  Finely shred the salad leaves. Slit open the pitta breads and fill with the salad. Push a few savoury bites into each pitta on top of the salad.

**Packing and storage**  Wrap in greaseproof paper or plastic wrap for transporting. Store the savoury bites in the refrigerator for up to 1 week.

## CHOCOLATE MUESLI FINGERS

• Makes 14 •

75 g (3 oz) polyunsaturated margarine
25 g (1 oz) soft dark brown sugar
15 ml (1 level tbsp) cocoa powder, sifted
15 ml (1 tbsp) runny honey
225 g (8 oz) no added sugar muesli

1  Grease an 18 cm (7 inch) square container. Heat the margarine, sugar, cocoa and honey in a heavy-based saucepan over a gentle heat until the margarine has melted and the sugar dissolved. Stir in the muesli and mix thoroughly together.

2  Spoon the mixture into the prepared container and level the surface. Chill in the refrigerator until set. When set, cut into 14 fingers.

**Packing and storage**  Wrap in foil or plastic wrap for transporting. Store in the refrigerator for up to 2 weeks.

## FRUITY VEGETABLE JUICE

• Serves 2 •

50 g (2 oz) desiccated coconut
2 carrots, scrubbed and grated
1 large eating apple, cored and chopped
juice of ½ lemon

1  Put the coconut into a jug, pour on 300 ml (½ pint) boiling water and stir well. Leave to stand for 30 minutes.

2  Purée the carrots, apple and lemon juice in a blender or food processor.

3  Strain the carrot and apple pulp through a sieve into a jug, then strain in the coconut milk. Chill in the refrigerator until ready for transporting.

**Packing and storage**  Pour into lidded containers for transporting. Store in the refrigerator for up to 1 day.

# FISHING

## MINI MUSHROOM QUICHES

• Makes 8 •

**For the pastry**
50 g (2 oz) plain wholemeal flour
50 g (2 oz) plain white flour
pinch of salt
50 g (2 oz) polyunsaturated margarine

**For the filling**
15 ml (1 tbsp) polyunsaturated margarine
1 small onion, skinned and chopped
50 g (2 oz) button mushrooms, sliced
25 g (1 oz) hard cheese, grated
150 ml ($\frac{1}{4}$ pint) milk
1 egg
5 ml (1 tsp) chopped fresh parsley
salt and pepper
thin button mushroom slices, to garnish

1 Lightly grease 8 barquette or boat-shaped moulds about 11.5 cm (4$\frac{1}{2}$ inches) in length, or 8 patty tins.

2 To make the pastry, put the flour and salt in a bowl. Rub in the margarine until the mixture resembles fine breadcrumbs. Add enough water to bind the ingredients and mix to form a smooth dough.

3 Roll out the dough on a lightly floured surface and use to line the prepared moulds or patty tins.

4 Melt the margarine in a small pan and fry the onions and mushrooms until soft. Allow to cool. Divide the filling between the moulds and top with the grated cheese.

5 Lightly whisk the milk, egg and parsley together. Season to taste with salt and pepper.

6 Spoon the mixture evenly over the mushroom and cheese filling. Garnish with the mushroom slices. Bake at 180°C (350°F) mark 4 for 20–25 minutes or until just set and golden brown. Transfer to a wire rack and leave to cool. Remove from the moulds.

**Packing and storage** Wrap in greaseproof paper or plastic wrap for transporting. Store in an airtight container for up to 2–3 days.

## TOMATO AND WATERCRESS SALAD

• Serves 4 •

1 large bunch of watercress, coarsely chopped
1 green eating apple, cored and chopped
15 ml (1 tbsp) lemon juice
225 g (8 oz) tomatoes, sliced or cut into wedges
30 ml (2 tbsp) olive oil
salt and pepper

1 Mix all the ingredients together in a bowl. Season to taste with salt and pepper.

**Packing and storage** Transfer to small lidded containers for transporting. Store in the refrigerator for up to 1 day.

## CHOCOLATE CUP CAKES

• Makes 12–14 •

100 g (4 oz) polyunsaturated margarine
100 g (4 oz) soft light brown sugar
50 g (2 oz) self-raising wholemeal flour
25 g (1 oz) self-raising white flour
25 g (1 oz) cocoa powder, sifted
pinch of baking powder
2 eggs

**For the chocolate fudgy topping**
75 g (3 oz) plain chocolate
25 g (1 oz) polyunsaturated margarine
75 g (3 oz) icing sugar, sifted
coloured sweets, to decorate

1 Spread 12–14 paper cake cases out on a baking sheet or put them in patty tins.

2 Put the margarine, sugar, flours, cocoa, baking powder and eggs into a bowl and beat together until smooth. Two-thirds fill the cases with the mixture.

**3** Bake at 190°C (375°F) mark 5 for 15 minutes or until well risen and firm to the touch. Transfer to a wire rack and leave to cool.

**4** To make the topping, break up the chocolate and melt with the margarine in a heatproof bowl over a pan of gently simmering water. Remove the bowl from the heat. Add the icing sugar and 30 ml (2 tbsp) warm water and beat well.

**5** Quickly spread the chocolate icing over the cup cakes. Decorate with sweets. Leave to set.

**Packing and storage** Wrap in plastic wrap or foil for transporting. Store in an airtight container for up to 3–4 days, or pack and freeze.

# STILL LEMONADE OR LIMEADE

• Serves 4 •

*3 large lemons or 6 large limes*
*30 ml (2 tbsp) runny honey*

**1** Finely grate the lemon or lime rind. Carefully peel the lemons or limes, making sure that all the bitter white pith is removed. Chop the flesh and discard any pips.

**2** Purée the lemon or lime rind, flesh, honey and 600 ml (1 pint) water in a blender or food processor until smooth. Strain the drink into a jug. Chill in the refrigerator until ready for transporting.

**Packing and storage** Pour into lidded beakers for transporting. Store in the refrigerator for up to

# TOBOGGANING

## SAUSAGE AND BACON KEBABS

• Serves 4 •

*4 rashers of streaky bacon, rinded and stretched*
*8 cocktail sausages*
*oil, for brushing*
*salt and pepper*

**1** Cut each bacon rasher in half and roll up. Thread a bacon roll and a sausage on to 8 wooden cocktail sticks or small bamboo skewers. Brush lightly with oil and season to taste with salt and pepper.

**2** Cook the kebabs under a hot grill for about 3–4 minutes each side or until the bacon and sausages are cooked and browned. Allow to cool. Store in the refrigerator until ready for transporting. Serve with lettuce, if liked.

**Packing and storage** Wrap in plastic wrap or foil for transporting. Store in the refrigerator for up to 1–2 days.

# Finger Rolls

• Makes 16 •

100 g (4 oz) strong wholemeal flour
100 g (4 oz) strong white flour
large pinch of salt
50 g (2 oz) polyunsaturated margarine
$\frac{1}{2}$ sachet of easy blend yeast
about 150 ml ($\frac{1}{4}$ pint) tepid milk
beaten egg yolk, to glaze

1  Grease a baking sheet. Put the flours and salt into a bowl. Rub in the margarine until the mixture resembles fine breadcrumbs. Add the yeast and mix well. Add the milk and mix to form a soft dough.

2  Knead dough on a lightly floured surface for 10 minutes until elastic and no longer sticky. Divide into sixteen pieces. Shape and place fairly close together on the prepared baking sheet. Cover with a clean tea-towel and leave in a warm place for about 30 minutes or until doubled in size.

3  Brush the rolls with glaze. Bake at 220°C (425°F) mark 7 for 15 minutes or until golden brown. Separate when cool.

**Packing and storage**  Wrap in plastic wrap or greaseproof paper for transporting. Store in an airtight container for up to 2 days, or freeze.

# Carrot and Peanut Soup

• Serves 4 •

15 ml (1 tbsp) coriander seeds, optional
5 ml (1 tsp) cumin seeds, optional
25 g (1 oz) polyunsaturated margarine
1 large onion, skinned and chopped
1 garlic clove, skinned and crushed
5 ml (1 level tsp) ground turmeric
450 g (1 lb) carrots, scrubbed and chopped
75 g (3 oz) American peanuts, chopped
600 ml (1 pint) hot vegetable stock
150 ml ($\frac{1}{4}$ pint) milk
salt and pepper
soured cream or natural yogurt, American
     peanuts and a little cayenne, to garnish

1  If using, crush the coriander seeds and cumin seeds in a pestle and mortar.

2  Melt the margarine in a large saucepan and gently fry the crushed spices, onion and garlic for a few minutes. Add the turmeric, carrots and peanuts and stir well. Cover and cook gently for 10 minutes before stirring in the stock. Bring to the boil, cover and simmer for 30 minutes.

3  Cool slightly, then purée the soup with the milk in a blender or food processor until very smooth (you may have to do this twice to break down the peanuts). Return to the rinsed-out pan, bring to the boil. Season to taste. Reheat for transporting.

**Packing and storage**  Pour into vacuum flasks for transporting. Store in the refrigerator for up to 1 week, or pack and freeze.

# Raspberry Trifles

• Serves 4 •

225 g (8 oz) fresh raspberries
45 ml (3 tbsp) fresh fruit juice
100 g (4 oz) chocolate sponge cake, finely
     crumbled
200 ml (7 fl oz) Greek strained yogurt
fresh raspberries, to decorate

1  Put the raspberries in a pan and simmer in the fruit juice for about 5 minutes or until soft. Leave to cool.

2  Put the cake crumbs into a bowl and stir in 45 ml (3 tbsp) of the yogurt.

3  Divide the sponge mixture between 4 individual containers. Spoon the raspberry mixture on top.

4  Spoon the remaining yogurt on top of the trifles. Chill in the refrigerator until ready for transporting. Decorate with raspberries.

**Packing and storage**  Cover the containers with a lid or plastic wrap for transporting. Best eaten on the day of making.

# EASTER BUNNY

## SMOKED MACKEREL PÂTÉ

• Serves 4 •

*350 g (12 oz) smoked mackerel fillets*
*50 g (2 oz) polyunsaturated margarine*
*30 ml (2 tbsp) natural yogurt*
*30 ml (2 tbsp) mayonnaise*
*pepper*
*grated rind and juice of ½ lemon*
*15 ml (1 tbsp) snipped chives*

1 Remove and discard the skin and any bones from the mackerel fillets. Purée the flesh in a blender or food processor with the remaining ingredients, except the chives. Stir in the chives. Put into 4 individual dishes.

**Packing and storage** Cover the dishes with plastic wrap for transporting. Store in the refrigerator for up to 3 days.

## PITTA BREAD FINGERS

• Serves 4 •

*2–3 large pitta breads*

1 Cut the pitta breads widthways into 2.5 cm (1 inch) fingers.

**Packing and storage** Wrap in greaseproof paper, paper napkins or plastic wrap for transporting. Best eaten on the day of making.

## PASTA AND SWEETCORN SALAD

• Serves 4 •

*100 g (4 oz) small dried red, green and white*
*pasta shapes*
*salt and pepper*
*30 ml (2 tbsp) olive oil*
*30 ml (2 tbsp) chopped fresh parsley*
*100 g (4 oz) sweetcorn kernels*
*1 small red pepper, seeded and diced*
*1 small green pepper, seeded and diced*

1 Cook the pasta in a saucepan of boiling salted water for 8–10 minutes or until just cooked. Drain thoroughly and put into a bowl.

2 Pour over the oil and stir in the remaining ingredients. Season to taste with salt and pepper and leave to cool.

**Packing and storage** Spoon into small lidded containers for transporting. Store in the refrigerator for up to 1 week.

## FRUIT AND NUT NIBBLES

• Makes about 18 •

*100 g (4 oz) sticky dried fruits, such as stoned*
*dates, figs, stoned prunes*
*100 g (4 oz) dried fruits, such as dried*
*apricots, pineapple or mango*
*25 g (1 oz) American peanuts*
*25 g (1 oz) desiccated coconut or 2 sheets rice*
*paper*

1 Process all the fruits and nuts in a food processor or medium cutter of a hand mincer until well mixed together.

2 Roll the mixture into about 18 balls (you may find it easy to have slightly wet hands). Roll each ball in coconut until coated all over. Alternatively, place the mixture between 2 sheets of rice paper and roll out until about 0.5 cm (¼ inch) thick. Using a sharp knife or scissors, cut into shapes or small bars.

**Packing and storage** Wrap in plastic wrap or foil for transporting. Store in the refrigerator for up to 1 week.

## BANANA SHAKE

• Serves 4 •

*568 ml (1 pint) milk*
*2 ripe bananas, sliced*

1 Purée the milk and bananas in a blender or food processor until smooth. Transfer the drink to a jug. Chill in the refrigerator until ready for transporting.

**Packing and storage** Pour into lidded beakers for transporting. Shake vigorously before drinking. Store in the refrigerator for up to 1 day.

# KITES

## CHEESY CRESS ROLL

• Makes 12 •

225 g (8 oz) strong wholemeal flour
225 g (8 oz) strong white flour
large pinch of salt
50 g (2 oz) polyunsaturated margarine
1 sachet of easy blend yeast
beaten egg yolk, to glaze
100 g (4 oz) hard cheese, grated
mustard and cress

**1** Grease a baking sheet. Put the flours and salt into a bowl and rub in the margarine. Add the yeast and mix well. Make a well in the centre, add about 300 ml (½ pint) tepid water and mix to a soft dough, adding a little water if necessary.

**2** Knead on a floured surface for 10 minutes until elastic and no longer sticky. Shape into twelve rolls. Place on baking sheet and cover with a clean tea-towel. Leave in a warm place for about 30 minutes or until doubled in size. Flatten the rolls slightly. Brush the rolls with glaze. Sprinkle over the cheese. Bake at 230°C (450°F) mark 8 for 15–20 minutes or until well risen and golden brown. Cool on a wire rack.

**Packing and storage**  Split, spread with a little polyunsaturated margarine and fill with mustard and cress. Wrap in plastic wrap or greaseproof paper for transporting. Store in an airtight container for up to 1–2 days, or wrap and freeze.

## SMOKED SAUSAGE AND PEANUT SALAD

• Serves 4 •

100 g (4 oz) smoked sausage, diced
1 large carrot, scrubbed and diced
3 celery sticks, trimmed and chopped
75 g (3 oz) American peanuts
1 green pepper, seeded and chopped
60 ml (4 tbsp) natural yogurt
45 ml (3 tbsp) mayonnaise
15 ml (1 tbsp) lemon juice
salt and pepper
celery leaves, to garnish

1  Mix the sausage, carrot, celery, peanuts and green pepper together in a bowl.

2  Mix the yogurt, mayonnaise and lemon juice together and season to taste with salt and pepper. Pour over the salad and toss lightly together. Chill in the refrigerator until ready for transporting. Garnish with celery leaves.

**Packing and storage**  Pack in small lidded containers for transporting. Store in the refrigerator for up to 2 days.

## PINEAPPLE AND COCONUT COCKTAIL

• Serves 4 •

75 ml (5 tbsp) desiccated coconut
4 slices of fresh pineapple, peeled, or 6 small
  canned pineapple rings in natural juice,
  drained
150 ml ($\frac{1}{4}$ pint) apple juice
150 ml ($\frac{1}{4}$ pint) orange juice
runny honey, to taste
selection of fresh fruit pieces, dipped in lemon
  juice, and shredded coconut, to decorate

1  Put the coconut in a jug with 300 ml ($\frac{1}{2}$ pint) boiling water. Leave to stand for 1 hour. Strain the coconut milk and chill for 1 hour.

2  Purée the pineapple and apple juice in a blender or food processor until smooth. Stir in the orange juice, coconut milk and honey to taste. Pour into a jug and chill in the refrigerator until ready for transporting.

3  To serve, thread the fruit pieces on to small wooden kebab sticks or cocktail sticks. Sprinkle the shredded coconut on top and serve with the drink.

**Packing and storage**  Pour into lidded beakers. Wrap the fruit sticks in foil or plastic wrap for transporting. Store in the refrigerator for up to 2 days.

## GINGERBREAD PEOPLE

• Makes 6 •

75 g (3 oz) plain wholemeal flour
75 g (3 oz) plain white flour
2.5 ml ($\frac{1}{2}$ level tsp) bicarbonate of soda
5 ml (1 level tsp) ground ginger
50 g (2 oz) polyunsaturated margarine
75 g (3 oz) soft light brown sugar
30 ml (2 tbsp) golden syrup, molasses or black
  treacle
30 ml (2 tbsp) beaten egg
currants, to decorate

1  Grease a baking sheet. Put the flours, bicarbonate of soda and ginger into a bowl. Rub in the margarine until the mixture resembles fine breadcrumbs. Stir in the sugar. Beat the syrup into the egg and stir into the flour mixture. Mix to form a dough and knead lightly until smooth.

2  Roll out the dough on a lightly floured surface to about 0.3 cm ($\frac{1}{8}$ inch) thick. Using a gingerbread person cutter, cut out figures and place on the prepared baking sheet. The smaller the cutter, the more gingerbread people the mixture will make. Decorate with currants.

3  Bake at 190°C (375°F) mark 5 for 10–15 minutes or until golden brown. Leave to cool on the baking sheet for a few minutes, then transfer to a wire rack and leave to cool completely.

**Packing and storage**  Wrap in plastic wrap, paper napkin or foil for transporting. Store in an airtight container for up to 3–4 days, or wrap and freeze.

# DINOSAURS

## SANDWICH SHAPES

• Serves 4 •

8 slices of wholemeal bread
polyunsaturated margarine, for spreading

For the crunchy cheese filling
50 g (2 oz) hard cheese, grated
I large carrot, scrubbed and grated
I small onion, skinned and grated
½ small red pepper, seeded and finely chopped
50 g (2 oz) natural quark
salt and pepper

For the egg and cress filling
2 hard-boiled eggs, chopped
30 ml (2 tbsp) mayonnaise
30 ml (2 tbsp) natural yogurt
mustard and cress
salt and pepper

1 Spread one side of each bread slice with the margarine.

2 Mix each filling separately and season to taste with salt and pepper.

3 Spread 2 slices of bread with the crunchy cheese mixture and two with the egg and cress. Top with the remaining slices of bread. Cut out plain or fancy shaped sandwiches using biscuit cutters. If liked, remove the top from each sandwich and use a smaller cutter to cut out the same shape to show the filling. Place back on top of the sandwich.

Packing and storage Wrap in greaseproof paper or plastic wrap for transporting. Store in the refrigerator for up to I day.

## MINI SAUSAGE ROLLS

• Makes about 16 •

75 g (3 oz) plain white flour
75 g (3 oz) plain wholemeal flour
pinch of salt
75 g (3 oz) polyunsaturated margarine
I egg
225 g (8 oz) lean pork sausagemeat
flour, for dusting
milk
beaten egg yolk, to glaze

1 To make the pastry, put the flours and salt in a bowl. Rub in the margarine until the mixture resembles fine breadcrumbs. Add the egg and mix to form a smooth dough.

2 Thinly roll out the dough on a lightly floured surface into an oblong about 15 cm (6 inches) wide and 30.5 cm (12 inches) long. Cut lengthways into 2 strips. Divide the sausagemeat into 2 pieces, dust with flour and form into 2 rolls the length of the pastry.

3 Lay a roll of sausagemeat down the centre of each strip. Brush the edges of the pastry with a little milk, fold one side of the pastry over the sausagemeat and press the 2 edges firmly together.

4 Brush the length of the 2 rolls with beaten egg yolk, then cut each into slices 4 cm (1½ inches) long. Make 3 diagonal cuts on the top of each sausage roll. Place on a baking sheet.

5 Bake at 200°C (400°F) mark 6 for 15 minutes. Reduce the oven temperature to 180°C (350°F) mark 4 and bake for a further 15 minutes. Allow to cool.

Packing and storage Wrap in greaseproof paper, plastic wrap or foil for transporting. Store in an airtight container for up to I week, or pack and freeze.

## CHOCOLATE PEANUT CRACKLES

• Makes about 12 •

15 ml (1 tbsp) runny honey
25 g (1 oz) polyunsaturated margarine
100 g (4 oz) plain chocolate
75 g (3 oz) bran flakes
50 g (2 oz) unsalted American peanuts
25 g (1 oz) sultanas

1 Put the honey, margarine and chocolate in a saucepan and stir over a low heat until melted. Remove from the heat.

2 Stir the bran flakes, peanuts and sultanas into the chocolate mixture and mix thoroughly until well coated. Spoon into individual paper cases. Leave in a cool place for about I hour or until set.

Packing and storage Wrap in plastic wrap or foil for transporting. Store in an airtight container for up to I week.

# LEMON BARLEY WATER

• Serves 4 •

*50 g (2 oz) pearl barley*
*finely grated rind and juice of 1 large lemon*
*15 ml (1 tbsp) runny honey*
*lemon slices, to decorate*

**1** Work the barley in a blender or food processor for 1 minute or until finely ground.

**2** Put the barley into a saucepan with the lemon rind and juice and 900 ml (1½ pints) cold water. Bring to the boil and simmer gently for 10 minutes, stirring occasionally.

**3** Strain the liquid into a jug and add the honey. Leave to cool. Chill in the refrigerator until ready for transporting. Decorate with lemon slices.

**Packing and storage** Pour into lidded beakers or vacuum flasks. Store in the refrigerator for up to 2 days.

# BACKPACK

## HUMMUS

• Serves 4 •

100 g (4 oz) dried chick peas soaked overnight,
   drained and rinsed, or 400 g (14 oz) can
   chick peas, drained and rinsed
1–2 garlic cloves, skinned and crushed
5 ml (1 level tsp) ground cumin
30 ml (2 tbsp) olive oil
45 ml (3 tbsp) lemon juice
45 ml (3 tbsp) tahini
30 ml (2 tbsp) natural yogurt
salt and pepper

1  If using dried beans, put them in a saucepan,
cover with cold water and bring to the boil.
Simmer for 1½ hours or until tender. Drain,
rinse well and leave to cool.

2  Puree all the ingredients in a blender or food
processor until smooth. Season to taste with
salt and pepper. Chill in the refrigerator until
ready for transporting.

**Packing and storage** Spoon into small lidded
containers for transporting. Store in the refrigerator
for up to 2–3 days.

## CRUNCHY VEGETABLE STICKS

• Serves 4 •

4 carrots, scrubbed
4 celery sticks, trimmed
½ cucumber
1 red pepper, seeded

1  Cut the vegetables into 5 cm (2 inch) long
sticks. Store in a polythene bag or airtight
container in the refrigerator until ready for
transporting.

**Packing and storage** Wrap a selection of the
vegetable sticks in plastic wrap for transporting.
Store in the refrigerator for up to 2 days.

# CHEESY VEGETABLE PIES

• Makes 12 •

**For the pastry**
150 g (5 oz) plain wholemeal flour
150 g (5 oz) plain white flour
150 g (5 oz) polyunsaturated margarine
50 g (2 oz) American peanuts, finely chopped
75 g (3 oz) hard cheese, finely grated

**For the filling**
1 small onion, skinned and finely chopped
1 medium potato, peeled and chopped
2 carrots, scrubbed and sliced
1 leek, washed, trimmed and thickly sliced
150 ml ($\frac{1}{4}$ pint) vegetable stock
25 g (1 oz) polyunsaturated margarine
30 ml (2 level tbsp) plain flour
200 ml (7 fl oz) milk
50 g (2 oz) hard cheese, grated
30 ml (2 tbsp) chopped fresh parsley
salt and pepper
beaten egg yolk, to glaze

1  Grease twelve patty tins and set aside. To make the pastry, put the flours in a bowl. Rub in the margarine until the mixture resembles fine breadcrumbs. Stir in the peanuts and 25 g (1 oz) of the cheese. Add enough water to bind the ingredients and mix to a smooth dough.

2  Using two-thirds of the pastry, roll out on a lightly floured surface, cut out twelve rounds using a 7.5 cm (3 inch) cutter and use to line the tins. Cover and chill while making the filling. Wrap the remaining pastry and chill until required.

3  For the filling, put the prepared vegetables in a saucepan. Pour on the stock and bring to the boil. Cover and simmer for 20–25 minutes or until tender. Drain the stock and reserve. Melt the margarine with the vegetables, add the flour and cook for 2–3 minutes. Remove from the heat and gradually add the cooking liquid and milk. Bring the sauce to the boil, stirring all the time until thickened, then simmer gently for 3 minutes. Stir in the cheese and parsley. Season to taste with salt and pepper and leave to cool.

4  Fill the pastry cases with the filling. Brush the edges with egg yolk. Roll out the remaining pastry and cut out twelve rounds using a 6.5 cm (2½ inch) fluted or plain cutter. If liked, remove the centre of each lid using a small shaped cutter to decorate. Place the lid on top and press well to seal. Brush the tops with egg yolk and sprinkle with the remaining cheese.

5  Bake at 200°C (400°F) mark 6 for 15–20 minutes or until the pastry is lightly browned. Leave to cool in the tins for a few minutes. Transfer to a wire rack and leave to cool completely.

**Packing and storage**  Wrap in plastic wrap, foil or paper napkin for transporting. Store in the refrigerator for up to 3 days, or wrap and freeze.

# ORANGE AND APPLE DRINK

• Serves 4 •

300 ml ($\frac{1}{2}$ pint) freshly squeezed orange juice
300 ml ($\frac{1}{2}$ pint) unsweetened apple juice
150–300 ml ($\frac{1}{4}$–$\frac{1}{2}$ pint) mineral water
orange shreds, to decorate

1  Mix all the ingredients together in a jug. Add the orange shreds. Chill in the refrigerator until ready for transporting.

**Packing and storage**  Pour into vacuum flasks or lidded plastic beakers for transporting. Store in the refrigerator for up to 1 week.

# FILM DIRECTOR

## CHEESY TRIANGLES

• Makes 12 •

**For the filling**
100 g (4 oz) low fat soft cheese, curd or ricotta
  cheese
15 ml (1 tbsp) lemon juice
1 small spring onion, trimmed
15 ml (1 tbsp) chopped fresh mixed herbs
salt and pepper

**For the pastry**
4 sheets of packet filo pastry, each measuring
  about 45.5 × 28 cm (18 × 11 inches)
75 g (3 oz) polyunsaturated margarine, melted
sesame seeds, for sprinkling

1 Grease a large baking sheet. To make the filling, beat together all ingredients and season to taste with salt and pepper.

2 Place one sheet of pastry on top of a second sheet and cut widthways into 6 double layer 7.5 cm (3 inch) strips. Repeat with the remaining 2 strips of pastry.

3 Brush the strips with melted margarine. Place a generous teaspoonful of filling at one end of each strip. Fold the filo pastry diagonally across the filling to form a triangle shape. Continue to fold, keeping the triangle shape until the end of the strip is reached. Repeat this until there are a total of twelve triangles.

4 Brush both sides of each triangle with the melted margarine.

5 Place in a single layer, seam side down, on the prepared baking sheet and sprinkle with sesame seeds. Bake at 220°C (425°F) mark 7 for 15 minutes or until golden brown. Transfer to a wire rack and leave to cool.

**Packing and storage** Wrap in paper napkin, plastic wrap or foil for transporting. Store in an airtight container for up to 3 days, or wrap and freeze at the end of stage 4.

## GREEK SALAD

• Serves 4 •

½ small cucumber
2 large tomatoes, sliced or cut into small
  wedges
50 g (2 oz) stoned black olives, optional
100 g (4 oz) feta cheese, crumbled
30–45 ml (2–3 tbsp) olive oil
salt and pepper
dried oregano

1 Peel off alternating strips of the cucumber skin lengthways, then slice the cucumber thickly and place in a bowl.

2 Add the tomatoes, olives and cheese and lightly mix together. Drizzle over the oil and season well with salt and pepper. Sprinkle with a little oregano. Chill in the refrigerator until ready for transporting.

**Packing and storage** Spoon into small lidded containers for transporting. Store in the refrigerator for up to 2 days.

## BANANA TARTS

• Makes 12 •

**For the pastry**
75 g (3 oz) plain white flour
75 g (3 oz) plain wholemeal flour
10 ml (2 level tsp) soft light brown sugar
pinch of salt
75 g (3 oz) polyunsaturated margarine

**For the filling**
1 large banana
1 egg
150 ml (¼ pint) natural yogurt
30 ml (2 level tbsp) soft light brown sugar
grated nutmeg
desiccated coconut, to decorate

1 Grease twelve patty tins. Put the flours, sugar and salt into a bowl. Rub in the margarine until the mixture resembles fine breadcrumbs. Add enough water to mix to a smooth dough.

2 Thinly roll out the dough. Cut out 12 rounds using a 7.5 cm (3 inch) fluted cutter. Cover and chill while making the filling.

3 Peel and mash the banana. Whisk the egg and yogurt together in a bowl and add the banana, 15 ml (1 tbsp) of the sugar and nutmeg.

4 Fill the pastry cases with the banana filling. Sprinkle generously with the desiccated coconut and remaining sugar. Bake at 190°C (375°F) mark 5 for 15–20 minutes or until the filling is firm to the touch and golden brown.

**Packing and storage** Wrap in plastic wrap or foil for transporting. Store in an airtight container for up to 3 days.

## PEACH COOLER

**• Serves 4 •**

**400 g (14 oz) can peaches in natural juice**
**300–450 ml ($\frac{1}{2}$–$\frac{3}{4}$ pint) pineapple juice**

**1** Purée the peaches and their juice in a blender or food processor until smooth. Stir in the pineapple juice. Pour the drink into a jug. Chill in the refrigerator until ready for transporting.

**Packing and storage** Pour into lidded plastic beakers for transporting. Store in the refrigerator for up to 1 week.

# AEROPLANE

## CHEESY BREAD PEOPLE

• Makes 2 •

4 large thin slices of bread
50 g (2 oz) Edam cheese, finely grated
50 g (2 oz) cottage cheese
pepper
thin cucumber slices

1 Using a small gingerbread person cutter, cut 4 shapes from the bread.

2 Mix the cheeses together with a little pepper and spread on to 2 of the shapes. Arrange a few cucumber slices on top. Top each with a second bread shape.

**Packing and storage** Wrap in greaseproof paper for transporting. Best eaten on the day of making.

## GRATED VEGETABLE SALAD

• Serves 2 •

3 carrots, scrubbed and coarsely grated
1 parsnip, peeled and coarsely grated
1 courgette, coarsely grated
10 ml (2 tsp) white wine vinegar
30 ml (2 tbsp) vegetable oil
2.5 ml ($\frac{1}{2}$ level tsp) dry mustard powder
salt and pepper

1 Mix all the ingredients together in a bowl. Season to taste with salt and pepper. Chill in the refrigerator until ready for transporting.

**Packing and storage** Spoon into small lidded containers for transporting. Store in the refrigerator for up to 3 days.

## CHERRY CAKE

• Makes 900 g (2 lb) loaf cake •

125 g (4 oz) polyunsaturated margarine
175 g (6 oz) self-raising white flour
75 g (3 oz) self-raising wholemeal flour
100 g (4 oz) desiccated coconut
125 g (4 oz) caster sugar
125 g (4 oz) red, green and yellow glacé
    cherries, halved
2 eggs
about 200 ml (7 fl oz) milk
shredded coconut

1 Grease a 900 g (2 lb) loaf tin and line the base with greaseproof paper.

2 Put the flours into a bowl and rub in the margarine until the mixture resembles fine breadcrumbs. Stir in the coconut, sugar and cherries. Make a well in the centre and beat in the eggs and enough milk to give a fairly soft dropping consistency.

3 Spoon the mixture into the prepared tin. Level the surface and scatter with shredded coconut. Bake at 180°C (350°F) mark 4 for 1$\frac{1}{2}$ hours or until a skewer inserted into the centre comes out clean. Cover with greaseproof paper if the cake browns too quickly. Turn out on to a wire rack and leave to cool.

**Packing and storage** Wrap slices in greaseproof paper, plastic wrap or paper napkins for transporting. Store in an airtight container for up to 1 week, or wrap and freeze.

## CHOCOLATE MILK

• Serves 2 •

20 ml (4 level tsp) cocoa powder
sugar, to taste
568 ml (1 pint) milk
grated chocolate

1 Dissolve the cocoa and sugar to taste in a little of the milk, then add the remainder. Chill in the refrigerator until ready for transporting. Sprinkle with grated chocolate to serve.

**Packing and storage** Pour into lidded beakers for transporting. Shake before serving. Store in the refrigerator for up to 1–2 days.

# PONY CLUB

## BEEF AND BARLEY SOUP

• Serves 4 •

1.4 litres (2½ pints) vegetable stock
1 bay leaf
700 g (1½ lb) braising steak, cut into small
  pieces
45 ml (3 level tbsp) pearl barley
1 large onion, skinned and chopped
1 carrot, scrubbed and chopped
2 leeks, washed, trimmed and chopped
1 large parsnip, peeled and chopped
salt and pepper
30 ml (2 tbsp) chopped fresh parsley

1  Put the stock, bay leaf and steak in a large
saucepan. Bring to the boil, cover and simmer
for 1½ hours or until the meat is tender. Skim
off any fat from the surface.

2  Add the remaining ingredients, cover and
simmer for a further 45 minutes–1 hour or
until the barley is tender. Season to taste with
salt and pepper. Stir in a little extra chopped
parsley, if liked.

**Packing and storage**  Pour into vacuum flasks for
transporting. Store in the refrigerator for up to
2 days, or pack in individual portions and freeze.

## FLOWERPOT BREAD

• Makes 6 •

450 g (1 lb) strong wholemeal flour
5 ml (1 level tsp) salt
25 g (1 oz) polyunsaturated margarine
1 sachet of easy blend yeast
40 g (1½ oz) bran
beaten egg yolk, to glaze
poppy seeds, for sprinkling

1  Choose 6 clean, new clay 7.5 cm (3 inch)
flowerpots. Before using for the first time,
grease them well and bake in a hot oven for
about 30 minutes. This stops the flowerpots
cracking and the loaves sticking. Leave to cool,
then grease again.

2  Put the flour and salt into a bowl and rub in
the margarine. Stir in the yeast and bran. Add
about 450 ml (¾ pint) tepid water and mix
thoroughly together to form a soft dough.

3  Turn out the dough on to a lightly floured
surface and knead for 10 minutes until elastic
and no longer sticky.

4  Divide the dough in 6 pieces and shape into
the flowerpots. Cover with a clean tea-towel
and leave to rise in a warm place for about 45
minutes or until the dough has risen to the top
of the flowerpots.

5  Uncover, brush with the egg yolk and
sprinkle with poppy seeds. Bake at 230°C
(450°F) mark 8 for 10 minutes, then reduce the
oven temperature to 200°C (400°F) mark 6 and
bake for a further 20–25 minutes or until well
risen and firm.

6  Carefully remove the bread from the
flowerpots. Brush the sides with egg yolk and
sprinkle evenly with poppy seeds. Return to
the oven and bake for a further 5–10 minutes or
until the sides are golden brown.

**Packing and storage**  Slice and spread with a little
polyunsaturated margarine, then wrap in plastic
wrap for transporting. Store in an airtight container
for up to 1–2 weeks, or wrap and freeze.

## POPCORN

• Serves 4 •

15 ml (1 tbsp) vegetable oil
50 g (2 oz) popping corn
little salt

1  Heat the oil in a large saucepan. Add the corn
and cover with a tight-fitting lid. Keep the heat
fairly high until the corn starts to pop.

2  Lower the heat slightly and continue to cook,
shaking the pan occasionally, for 2–3 minutes or
until the popping stops. Season with a little
salt.

**Packing and storage**  Transport in small lidded
containers or plastic bags. Alternatively, make small
paper cones from semicircular pieces of thin card,
secure with sticky tape, then fill with the corn. Wrap
in plastic wrap for transporting. Store in an airtight
container for up to 2–3 days.

# ORANGE FRUIT CUP

• Serves 4 •

**4 large oranges**
**225 g (8 oz) fresh fruit in season, such**
**as apples, grapes, strawberries,**
**cherries, finely chopped**

**1** Cut a thick slice from the top of each orange and reserve. Using a teaspoon, scoop out the inside of the oranges.

**2** Cut a thin slice from the base of each orange so that it stands up straight.

**3** Squeeze the juice from the scooped out orange flesh and mix with the fresh fruit. Pile into the orange shells and replace the lids.

**Packing and storage** Wrap in plastic wrap for transporting. Store in the refrigerator overnight. Best eaten within 1 day of making.

# SCHOOL TIME

## CREAMY CHICKEN IN PITTA POCKETS

• Serves 2 •

225 g (8 oz) cooked chicken, skinned
2 celery sticks, trimmed and chopped
1 green eating apple, cored and roughly
    chopped
50 g (2 oz) American peanuts
45 ml (3 tbsp) mayonnaise
30 ml (2 tbsp) natural yogurt
pepper
2 pitta breads
Cos lettuce leaves

**1** Cut the chicken into bite-sized pieces. Mix the chicken, celery and apple with the peanuts.

**2** Beat the mayonnaise and yogurt together, then pour over the chicken mixture. Toss together to coat in the dressing, then season to taste with pepper.

**3** Cut the pitta bread in half and open up to make a pocket. Tuck a few lettuce leaves into each, then pile in the chicken mixture.

**Packing and storage** Wrap in plastic wrap for transporting. Store the chicken filling in the refrigerator for up to 2–3 days.

## GREEN GRAPE SALAD

• Serves 2 •

225 g (8 oz) seedless green grapes, halved
½ small red pepper, seeded and chopped
¼ cucumber, chopped
few beansprouts
15 ml (1 tbsp) vegetable oil
15 ml (1 tbsp) lemon juice
salt and pepper

1 Mix the grapes, red pepper, cucumber and beansprouts together in a bowl.

2 Whisk the oil and lemon juice together and season to taste with salt and pepper. Pour over the salad.

**Packing and storage** Pack into small lidded containers for transporting. Store in the refrigerator for up to 2 days.

## MARBLED FUDGE BARS

• Makes 12 •

75 g (3 oz) plain chocolate
100 g (4 oz) polyunsaturated margarine
175 g (6 oz) caster sugar
3 eggs
75 g (3 oz) plain wholemeal flour
vanilla flavouring
100 g (4 oz) low fat soft cheese

1 Grease and line an 18 × 18 cm (7 × 7 inch) baking tin.

2 Break the chocolate into squares and place in a large heatproof bowl with the margarine. Stand the bowl over a saucepan of simmering water and stir until the chocolate has melted.

3 Add 100 g (4 oz) of the sugar, 2 of the eggs, the flour and a few drops of vanilla flavouring. Beat the mixture together and pour into the prepared tin.

4 Beat together the cheese with the remaining sugar and egg and a few drops of vanilla flavouring. Spoon on top of the chocolate mixture. Pull a knife through the 2 mixtures to give a marbled effect.

5 Bake at 180°C (350°F) mark 4 for 45 minutes or until firm to the touch. Leave to cool in the tin, then cut into twelve small bars.

**Packing and storage** Wrap in greaseproof paper or plastic wrap for transporting. Store in an airtight container for up to 1 week, or wrap and freeze.

## CARIBBEAN QUENCHER

• Serves 2 •

300 ml (½ pint) pineapple juice
150 ml (¼ pint) tropical fruit juice
150 ml (¼ pint) mineral water
few lime slices

1 Mix all the ingredients together in a jug. Chill in the refrigerator until ready for transporting.

**Packing and storage** Pour into vacuum flasks or lidded plastic beakers for transporting. Store in the refrigerator for up to 1 week.

# MINIATURE GARDEN

## CLUB SANDWICHES

• Serves 2 •

6 rashers of streaky bacon, rinded
6 slices of bread
mayonnaise, for spreading
lettuce leaves
2 large slices of cooked turkey or chicken
2 small tomatoes, sliced

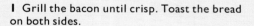

1 Grill the bacon until crisp. Toast the bread on both sides.

2 Spread one side of each slice of toast with a little mayonnaise. Arrange a few lettuce leaves on 2 slices and top each with a slice of turkey. Place a slice of toast on top, mayonnaise side up. Arrange a few lettuce leaves, the bacon and tomato slices on top. Cover with the remaining slices of toast, mayonnaise side down.

3 Cut the sandwiches diagonally into quarters.

**Packing and storage** Wrap in greaseproof paper for transporting. Best eaten on the day of making.

## POTATO SALAD

• Serves 2 •

225 g (8 oz) very small new potatoes, halved
salt
45 ml (3 tbsp) set natural yogurt
50 g (2 oz) American dry roasted peanuts, finely chopped
5 ml (1 tsp) Dijon mustard
paprika

1 Cook the potatoes in a saucepan of boiling salted water for about 15 minutes until tender. Drain.

2 Beat the yogurt, peanuts and mustard together and season with a little paprika. Pour over the potatoes and toss together. Chill in the refrigerator until ready for transporting.

**Packing and storage** Spoon into small lidded containers for transporting. Store in the refrigerator for up to 2–3 days.

## POLKA DOT MUFFINS

• Makes 12 •

50 g (2 oz) polyunsaturated margarine
200 ml (7 fl oz) milk
1 egg
175 g (6 oz) soft light brown sugar
225 g (8 oz) polka dots
pinch of salt
225 g (8 oz) self-raising white flour
125 g (4 oz) self-raising wholemeal flour

1 Line twelve deep muffin tins with paper cases. Melt the margarine in a small saucepan. Pour into a large bowl, then beat in the remaining ingredients.

2 Spoon the mixture into the paper cases. Bake at 220°C (425°F) mark 7 for 20–25 minutes or until well risen and firm to the touch.

**Packing and storage** Split and spread with a little polyunsaturated margarine. Wrap in plastic wrap or paper napkin for transporting. Store in an airtight container for up to 1 day, or wrap and freeze.

# STRAWBERRY SHAKE

• Serves 2 •

*150 ml (¼ pint) thin natural yogurt*
*juice of 1 large orange*
*50 g (2 oz) ripe strawberries, hulled*
*honey, to taste*
*few strawberries, to decorate*

**1** Purée all the ingredients in a blender or food processor until smooth. Float a few strawberries on the top. Chill in the refrigerator until ready for transporting.

**Packing and storage** Pour into lidded beakers or vacuum flasks. Shake before drinking. Store in the refrigerator for up to 1–2 days.

# BIKE

## ALPHABET SOUP

• Serves 4 •

2 leeks, washed, trimmed and sliced
3 carrots, scrubbed and sliced
1 bouquet garni
750 ml (1¼ pints) chicken stock
1 chicken quarter
40 g (1½ oz) alphabet pasta shapes
50 g (2 oz) frozen peas
30 ml (2 tbsp) chopped fresh parsley
salt and pepper

**1** Put the leeks, carrots, bouquet garni, stock and chicken in a large saucepan. Bring to the boil, cover and simmer for 20–30 minutes or until the chicken is tender.

**2** Remove the chicken, then add the pasta and peas. Bring back to the boil and simmer for 10–15 minutes or until the pasta is tender.

**3** Meanwhile, discard the skin and bone from the chicken and cut the flesh into small pieces. Return the chicken to the soup with the parsley. Season to taste with salt and pepper.

**Packing and storage** Pour into vacuum flasks for transporting. Store in the refrigerator for up to 1–2 days.

## TUNA SALAD

• Serves 4 •

6 new potatoes, boiled
salt and pepper
2 hardboiled eggs
½ iceberg lettuce
3 ripe tomatoes
¼ cucumber
198 g (7 oz) can tuna in brine, drained
100 g (4 oz) French beans, cooked and halved
15 ml (1 tbsp) lemon juice
30 ml (2 tbsp) vegetable oil
30 ml (2 tbsp) mayonnaise

1 Cut the lettuce, tomatoes and cucumber into bite-sized pieces. Flake the tuna and mix with the salad ingredients.

2 Chop the potatoes and the eggs. Mix into the salad with the French beans. Season and chill.

3 Just before packing, whisk the lemon juice, oil and mayonnaise together and pour over the salad.

**Packing and storage** Spoon into small lidded containers for transporting. Store undressed salad in the refrigerator for up to 1–2 days.

## HERBY BAPS

• Makes about 12 •

225 g (8 oz) strong wholemeal flour
225 g (8 oz) strong white flour
salt
25 g (1 oz) polyunsaturated margarine
45 ml (3 tbsp) chopped fresh parsley and
   chives
1 sachet of easy blend yeast

1 Grease 2–3 baking sheets. Put the flours and salt in a bowl and rub in the margarine. Stir in the herbs, yeast and about 300 ml (½ pint) tepid water to give a fairly soft dough.

2 Turn out the dough on to a floured surface and knead for about 10 minutes until elastic and no longer sticky. Shape into about twelve baps and place on the baking sheets. Cover and leave in a warm place until doubled in size.

3 Dredge the tops of the baps lightly with flour. Bake at 200°C (400°F) mark 6 for 15–20 minutes. Transfer to a wire rack to cool.

**Packing and storage** Split and spread with a little polyunsaturated margarine, then wrap in plastic wrap or greaseproof paper for transporting. Store in an airtight container for up to 1–2 days or wrap and freeze.

## CRUNCHY PEANUT COOKIES

• Makes about 20 •

125 g (4 oz) polyunsaturated margarine
125 g (4 oz) soft brown sugar
60 ml (4 tbsp) crunchy peanut butter
100 g (4 oz) plain wholemeal flour
100 g (4 oz) plain white flour
2.5 ml (1 level tsp) baking powder
runny honey, to glaze
50 g (2 oz) American peanuts, chopped

1 Cream the margarine and sugar together in a bowl until smooth. Mix in the peanut butter, flours and baking powder, then add about 30 ml (2 tbsp) water to make a soft dough.

2 Roll out the dough on a lightly floured surface until fairly thin. Cut into shapes using cutters. Re-knead the trimmings and repeat to make about twenty cookies.

3 Arrange the cookies on a baking sheet. Brush with a little honey to glaze, then sprinkle with the peanuts. Bake at 190°C (375°F) mark 5 for 15–20 minutes or until golden brown. Transfer to a wire rack and leave to cool.

**Packing and storage** Wrap in paper napkin for transporting. Store in an airtight container for up to 1–2 weeks, or pack and freeze.

# ODDS AND ENDS

# SOUPS

## FISH CHOWDER

• Serves 4 •

350 g (12 oz) white fish fillet or smoked fish
  fillet
5 ml (1 tsp) lemon juice
1 bouquet garni
1 bay leaf
salt and pepper
25 g (1 oz) polyunsaturated margarine
1 small onion, skinned and chopped
1 small green pepper, seeded and diced
25 g (1 oz) plain white flour
450 ml ($\frac{3}{4}$ pint) milk
1 large carrot, scrubbed and grated
1 medium potato, peeled and diced
198 g (7 oz) can sweetcorn kernels, drained
30 ml (2 tbsp) chopped fresh parsley

1  Put the fish in a saucepan with 150 ml ($\frac{1}{4}$ pint) water, the lemon juice, bouquet garni and bay leaf. Season. Poach for 10–15 minutes. Strain and reserve the cooking liquid, then flake the fish, discarding any skin and bones.

2  Melt the margarine in a saucepan and gently fry the onion and green pepper until soft. Stir in the flour and cook for 2 minutes, stirring all the time. Remove from the heat and gradually stir in the reserved fish stock and milk. Bring to the boil, stirring until thickened. Add the carrot and potato. Simmer for 15 minutes.

3  Stir in the fish, sweetcorn and parsley.

Season and heat gently until hot.

**Packing and storage**  Pour into vacuum flasks for transporting. Store in the refrigerator for up to 3 days, or pack and freeze.

## CREAMY CHICKEN SOUP

• Serves 4 •

25 g (1 oz) polyunsaturated margarine
1 large onion, skinned and finely chopped
25 g (1 oz) plain white flour
600 ml (1 pint) chicken stock
300 ml ($\frac{1}{2}$ pint) milk
salt and pepper
grated nutmeg
175 g (6 oz) cooked chicken, skinned and diced
5 ml (1 tsp) lemon juice
60 ml (4 tbsp) single cream
15 ml (1 tbsp) chopped fresh parsley

1  Melt the margarine in a large saucepan and fry the onion for 5 minutes until softened. Stir in the flour and cook for 2–3 minutes, stirring all the time. Remove from the heat and stir in the stock and milk, then season to taste with salt, pepper and nutmeg. Bring to the boil, cover and simmer gently for 15 minutes.

2  Stir in the chicken, lemon juice and cream. Reheat without boiling. Stir in the chopped parsley.

**Packing and storage**  Pour into vacuum flasks for transporting. Store in the refrigerator for up to 3 days. If freezing, freeze before adding the cream, then add when reheating.

## CREAM OF MUSHROOM SOUP

• Serves 4 •

225 g (8 oz) mushrooms, sliced
1 large onion, skinned and chopped
300 ml ($\frac{1}{2}$ pint) vegetable stock
25 g (1 oz) polyunsaturated margarine
40 g ($1\frac{1}{2}$ oz) plain white flour
450 ml ($\frac{3}{4}$ pint) milk
salt and pepper
15 ml (1 tbsp) chopped fresh parsley
30 ml (2 tbsp) single cream or Greek strained
  yogurt

1  Put the mushrooms, onion and stock in a saucepan. Bring to the boil, cover and simmer for 30 minutes. Cool slightly, then purée in a blender or food processor until smooth.

2  Melt the margarine in the rinsed-out saucepan, stir in the flour and cook for 2 minutes, stirring all the time. Remove from the heat and gradually stir in the milk. Bring to the boil, stirring until thickened.

3  Stir in the mushroom purée and season to taste with salt and pepper. Simmer for 15 minutes. Allow to cool slightly, then stir in the parsley and cream. Reheat without boiling. Serve hot.

**Packing and storage**  Pour into vacuum flasks for transporting. Store in the refrigerator for up to 3 days, or pack and freeze.

## LENTIL AND BACON SOUP

• Serves 4 •

75 g (3 oz) red lentils, washed
900 ml (1½ pints) vegetable stock
1 large onion, skinned and chopped
4 lean rashers of bacon, rinded and chopped
198 g (7 oz) can tomatoes
15 ml (1 tbsp) tomato purée
salt and pepper
15 ml (1 tbsp) chopped fresh parsley

1 Put the lentils, stock, onion, bacon, tomatoes and tomato purée in a large saucepan. Season to taste with salt and pepper. Bring to the boil, cover and simmer for about 1 hour or until the lentils are soft.

2 Cool slightly, then purée the soup in a blender or food processor until smooth. Stir in the parsley. Reheat and adjust the seasoning if necessary.

**Packing and storage** Pour into vacuum flasks for transporting. Store in the refrigerator for up to 1 week, or pack and freeze.

# SPREADS & FILLINGS

## HONEY CHEESE SPREAD

• Makes enough for 4–6 sandwiches •

225 g (8 oz) low fat soft cheese, curd cheese or cottage cheese, sieved
30 ml (2 tbsp) crunchy peanut butter
15 ml (1 tbsp) runny honey
15 ml (1 tbsp) natural yogurt

1 Purée all the ingredients in a blender or food processor until smooth. Chill in the refrigerator until ready for transporting. Use as a sandwich filler.

**Storage** Store in the refrigerator for up to 3 days.

## HERBY NUT SPREAD

• Serves 4 •

100 g (4 oz) dried butter beans, soaked overnight, drained and rinsed, or 396 g (14 oz) can butter beans, drained and rinsed
30 ml (2 tbsp) olive oil
finely grated rind and juice of 1 lemon
45 ml (3 tbsp) crunchy wholenut peanut butter
45 ml (3 tbsp) chopped fresh parsley or coriander
salt and pepper

1 Put the beans in a saucepan, cover with cold water and bring to the boil. Simmer for

1½ hours or until tender. Drain and rinse well.

2 Purée the beans, oil, lemon rind and juice, peanut butter and herbs in a blender or food processor until smooth. Season to taste with salt and pepper. Chill in the refrigerator until ready for transporting.

**Packing and storage** Transfer to small lidded containers for transporting. Store in the refrigerator for up to 3 days.

## NUTTY CHOCOLATE DIP

• Serves 4–6 •

125 g (4 oz) chocolate, milk or plain
30 ml (2 tbsp) golden syrup
30 ml (2 tbsp) peanut butter
30 ml (2 tbsp) milk
segments of fruit for dipping (satsuma, apple, banana, pear, strawberry, peach, pineapple)

1 Break up the chocolate and place in a pan with all the remaining ingredients. Heat gently, stirring all the time, until it forms a smooth sauce.

2 Pour the mixture into a small bowl and place in the centre of a plate. Surround with segments of fruit and spear on to forks to dip. Serve the dip warm.

**Packing and storage** Pour into a wide-necked vacuum flask for transporting. Store in the refrigerator for up to 3 days.

# BREADS & ROLLS

## PITTA BREAD FILLINGS

### Breakfast filling
Mix chopped hard-boiled eggs with chopped crisp grilled bacon and sliced tomatoes. Bind with a little mayonnaise.

### Prawn Cocktail Filling
Mix cooked peeled prawns with shredded lettuce and cucumber. Spoon over a little mayonnaise flavoured with tomato purée, mustard and lemon juice.

### Beefy Beef Filling
Thinly slice roast beef and spread with a little horseradish or mustard for older children. Use to fill a lettuce-lined pitta.

### Sausage and Pickle Filling
Chop cold cooked sausages and mix with home-made chutney or pickle. Pack into pitta with thinly sliced apple and chopped celery.

### Curried Chicken and Apricot Filling
Mix chopped cooked chicken with no-soak dried apricots, sultanas and green pepper. Bind together with natural yogurt flavoured with curry paste, mango chutney and lime or lemon juice.

### Hawaiian Dream Filling
Chop lean ham and hard cheese into chunks. Mix with fresh or canned pineapple chunks. Top with chopped spring onions.

### Banana Split Filling
Chop bananas and toss in lemon juice. Mix with chopped stoned dates or prunes. Bind together with natural yogurt flavoured with honey and toasted flaked almonds.

## PEANUT AND RAISIN BREAD

• Makes a 900 g (2 lb) loaf •

*225 g (8 oz) strong wholemeal flour*
*225 g (8 oz) strong white flour*
*pinch of salt*
*50 g (2 oz) polyunsaturated margarine*
*1 sachet of easy blend yeast*
*50 g (2 oz) raisins*
*50 g (2 oz) American peanuts, roughly chopped*
*50 g (2 oz) candied mixed peel*
*1 egg*
*60 ml (4 tbsp) runny honey*
*150 ml ($\frac{1}{4}$ pint) tepid milk*
*milk, to glaze*
*chopped American peanuts, to decorate*

1  Grease a 900 g (2 lb) loaf tin. Put the flours and salt into a bowl and rub in the margarine. Stir in the yeast, raisins, peanuts and mixed peel.

2  Beat the egg and 45 ml (3 tbsp) of the honey together in a measuring jug, then make up to 150 ml ($\frac{1}{4}$ pint) with water. Pour in the tepid milk and mix thoroughly together. Add the liquid to the dry ingredients and mix to form a soft dough.

3  Turn out the dough on to a lightly floured surface and knead for 10 minutes until elastic and no longer sticky.

4  Divide the dough into 4 pieces and roll each piece into a ball. Place side by side in the prepared loaf tin and press down gently. Cover with a clean tea-towel and leave to rise in a warm place for about 45 minutes or until doubled in size.

5  Uncover, brush the tops lightly with milk and sprinkle with chopped peanuts. Bake at 220°C (425°F) mark 7 for 10 minutes, then reduce the oven temperature to 190°C (375°F) mark 5 and bake for a further 30–35 minutes until well risen and firm. Turn out on to a wire rack and leave to cool.

**Packing and storage**  Slice and spread with a little polyunsaturated margarine. Wrap slices in plastic wrap for transporting. Store in an airtight container for up to 3–4 days, or wrap and freeze.

## THREE SEED AND NUT ROLLS

• Makes about 12 •

*225 g (8 oz) strong wholemeal flour*
*225 g (8 oz) strong white flour*
*salt*
*25 g (1 oz) polyunsaturated margarine*
*1 sachet of easy blend yeast*
*30 ml (2 tbsp) sunflower seeds*
*15 ml (1 tbsp) poppy seeds*
*15 ml (1 tbsp) sesame seeds*
*50 g (2 oz) American peanuts, finely chopped*
*beaten egg yolk, to glaze*
*poppy seeds, sesame seeds or finely chopped American peanuts, to decorate*

1 Grease 2 baking sheets. Put the flours and salt into a bowl, then rub in the margarine. Stir in the yeast, sunflower seeds, poppy seeds, sesame seeds and peanuts. Add about 300 ml (½ pint) tepid water to give a fairly soft dough.

2 Turn out the dough on to a floured surface and knead for about 10 minutes until elastic and no longer sticky. Shape into about twelve rolls (or make into smaller baps if preferred). Place on the prepared baking sheets. Flatten the rolls slightly and snip 6 evenly spaced 0.5 cm (¼ inch) cuts in the edge of each roll. Cover with a clean tea-towel and leave in a warm place until doubled in size.

3 Brush each roll with egg yolk and sprinkle with poppy seeds, sesame seeds or finely chopped peanuts. Bake at 190°C (375°F) mark 5 for 15 minutes or until well risen and golden brown. Transfer to a wire rack and leave to cool.

**Packing and storage** Split and spread with a little polyunsaturated margarine. Wrap in plastic wrap or paper napkins for transporting. Store in an airtight container for up to 2 days, or wrap and freeze.

## FRUITY TEABREAD

• Makes a 900 g (2 lb) teabread •

*350 g (12 oz) mixed raisins, sultanas and*
*currants*
*175 g (6 oz) soft dark brown sugar*
*300 ml (½ pint) cold milkless tea*
*75 g (3 oz) honey-roasted American peanuts,*
*chopped*
*225 g (8 oz) self-raising wholemeal flour*
*5 ml (1 level tsp) ground mixed spice*
*1 egg*

1 Put the fruit, sugar and tea in a large bowl. Cover and leave to soak overnight.

2 Grease a 900 g (2 lb) loaf tin and line the base with greaseproof paper.

3 The next day add the remaining ingredients to the fruit mixture and beat thoroughly together. Spoon into the prepared loaf tin and level the surface. Bake at 180°C (350°F) mark 4 for 1¼ hours or until a skewer inserted into the centre comes out clean.

4 Turn out on to a wire rack and leave to cool. Wrap in greaseproof paper and foil and keep for 2 days before eating.

**Packing and storage** Slice and spread with a little polyunsaturated margarine. Wrap in plastic wrap for transporting. Store in an airtight container for up to 1–2 weeks, or wrap and freeze.

## FRUITY MALT LOAF

• Makes a 900 g (2 lb) loaf •

*175 g (6 oz) plain wholemeal flour*
*175 g (6 oz) plain white flour*
*5 ml (1 level tsp) baking powder*
*2.5 ml (½ level tsp) bicarbonate of soda*
*250 g (9 oz) mixed dried fruit*
*25 g (1 oz) soft light brown sugar*
*120 ml (8 tbsp) malt extract*
*2 eggs*
*225 ml (8 fl oz) milk*

1 Grease and base line a 900 g (2 lb) loaf tin. Grease a baking sheet. Put the flours, baking powder, bicarbonate of soda and 225 g (8 oz) of the fruit in a bowl and mix well together.

2 Put the sugar and malt extract in a saucepan and heat gently. Do not boil. Leave to cool slightly, then add to the dry ingredients with the eggs and milk. Beat well.

3 Spoon the mixture into the prepared tin and sprinkle with the remaining fruit. Cover with the baking sheet and place a weight on top. Bake at 150°C (300°F) mark 2 for about 1–1½ hours.

4 Turn out on to a wire rack and leave to cool. Wrap in greaseproof paper and keep for 2 days before eating.

**Packing and storage** Slice and spread with a little polyunsaturated margarine. Wrap in plastic wrap or greaseproof paper for transporting. Store in an airtight container for up to 1 week, or wrap and freeze.

# CAKES & BISCUITS

## GINGERBREAD

• Makes an 18 cm (7 inch) cake •

*100 g (4 oz) plain wholemeal flour*
*100 g (4 oz) plain white flour*
*large pinch of salt*
*10 ml (2 level tsp) ground ginger*
*7.5 ml (1½ level tsp) baking powder*
*2.5 ml (½ level tsp) bicarbonate of soda*
*100 g (4 oz) soft light brown sugar*
*75 g (3 oz) polyunsaturated margarine*
*75 g (3 oz) black treacle*
*75 g (3 oz) golden syrup*
*1 egg, size 6*
*150 ml (¼ pint) milk*

1  Grease and line a deep 18 cm (7 inch) square tin. Mix all the dry ingredients in a large bowl.

2  Put the sugar, margarine, treacle and syrup into a saucepan and heat gently over a low heat until melted. Do not boil. Leave to cool slightly.

3  Beat together the egg and milk and mix with the melted margarine mixture. Add to the dry ingredients and mix very thoroughly.

4  Turn the mixture into the prepared tin. Bake at 170°C (325°F) mark 3 for about 1–1½ hours or until firm to the touch. Turn out on to a wire rack and leave to cool. Wrap in greaseproof paper and foil and keep for a few days before eating.

**Packing and storage**  Cut into pieces and wrap in plastic wrap, greaseproof paper or paper napkins for transporting. Store in an airtight container or wrap in greaseproof paper for up to 1 week.

## DOUBLE CHOCOLATE CAKE

• Makes a 15 cm (6 inch) cake •

*40 g (1½ oz) self-raising wholemeal flour*
*40 g (1½ oz) self-raising white flour*
*30 ml (2 level tbsp) ground rice*
*100 g (4 oz) plain chocolate*
*100 g (4 oz) polyunsaturated margarine*
*75 g (3 oz) soft light brown sugar*
*few drops vanilla flavouring*
*2 eggs, beaten*

**For the icing**
*200 g (7 oz) plain chocolate, grated*
*75 g (3 oz) polyunsaturated margarine*

1  Grease and line a 15 cm (6 inch) cake tin. Mix the flours and ground rice together.

2  Break the chocolate into a heatproof bowl and place over a saucepan of simmering water. Stir until the chocolate has melted.

3  Cream the margarine, sugar and vanilla flavouring together in a bowl until pale and fluffy. Add the melted chocolate and mix lightly together. Beat in the egg, a little at a time. Fold in the flour mixture.

4  Spoon the mixture into the prepared tin. Bake at 180°C (350°F) mark 4 for about 1–1¼ hours or until a fine skewer inserted into the centre comes out clean. Turn out on to a wire rack and leave to cool.

5  To make the topping, break 150 g (5 oz) of the chocolate into small pieces and place in a heatproof bowl with the margarine and 30 ml (2 tbsp) water. Melt as before, then pour over the cooled cake, working quickly to cover the top and sides of the cake. Leave to set for about 1 hour.

6  Melt the remaining chocolate as before. Spoon into a small greaseproof paper piping bag, snip off the tip end and drizzle the chocolate over the cake to decorate. Leave to set.

**Packing and storage**  Wrap slices in plastic wrap, greaseproof paper, foil or a paper napkin for transporting. Store in an airtight container for up to 4 days, or wrap and freeze before covering with the icing.

## CARROT CAKE

• Makes a 20.5 cm (8 inch) cake •

*225 ml (8 fl oz) vegetable oil*
*225 g (8 oz) soft light brown sugar*
*225 g (8 oz) self-raising wholemeal flour*
*5 ml (1 level tsp) baking powder*
*5 ml (1 level tsp) ground mixed spice*
*450 g (1 lb) carrots, scrubbed and coarsely grated*
*finely grated rind of 1 lemon*
*15 ml (1 tbsp) lemon juice*
*100 g (4 oz) walnut halves, roughly chopped*
*walnut halves, to decorate*

1 Grease and base line a 20.5 cm (8 inch) round cake tin. Put all the ingredients in a bowl and beat thoroughly until well mixed. Spoon the mixture into the prepared tin and level the surface. Decorate with walnut halves.

2 Bake at 180°C (350°F) mark 4 for about 1½ hours or until well risen and golden brown. If over-browning, cover with greaseproof paper. Turn out on to a wire rack and leave to cool.

**Packing and storage** Wrap slices in plastic wrap, a paper napkin or foil for transporting. Store in an airtight container for up to 1 week.

## NUTTY FRUITCAKE

• Makes a 20 cm (8 inch) cake •

*100 g (4 oz) raisins*
*100 g (4 oz) sultanas*
*100 g (4 oz) stoned prunes, chopped*
*300 ml (½ pint) orange juice*
*100 g (4 oz) self-raising wholemeal flour*
*100 g (4 oz) self-raising white flour*
*2.5 ml (½ level tsp) baking powder*
*100 g (4 oz) chopped mixed nuts, such as American peanuts, walnuts, Brazil nuts or cashews*
*10 ml (2 level tsp) ground mixed spice*
*100 g (4 oz) polyunsaturated margarine*
*75 g (3 oz) soft dark brown sugar*
*2 eggs*
*selection of nuts, to decorate*

1 Grease and base line a deep 20 cm (8 inch) round cake tin. Put the dried fruit and 200 ml (⅓ pint) of the orange juice in a large bowl and leave to soak overnight.

2 Add the remaining ingredients and about 50 ml (2 fl oz) more orange juice to make a soft dropping consistency. Beat thoroughly together.

3 Spoon the mixture into the prepared tin and level the surface. Arrange nuts on top to decorate. Bake at 170°C (325°F) mark 3 for about 1 hour or until a fine skewer inserted into the centre comes out clean. If the cake browns quickly, cover with several layers of greaseproof paper.

4 Leave to cool in the tin for 15 minutes, then turn out on to a wire rack. Prick the base of the cake with a fine skewer and spoon over about 30 ml (2 tbsp) of the remaining orange juice. Leave to cool completely.

**Packing and storage** Wrap slices in greaseproof paper, plastic wrap, foil or a paper napkin for transporting. Store in an airtight container for several weeks.

## ROCK BUNS

• Makes 16 •

*100 g (4 oz) self-raising wholemeal flour*
*100 g (4 oz) self-raising white flour*
*salt*
*2.5 ml (½ level tsp) ground mixed spice*
*grated nutmeg*
*100 g (4 oz) polyunsaturated margarine*
*75 g (3 oz) soft light brown sugar*
*100 g (4 oz) stoned chopped dates or mixed dried fruit*
*grated rind of ½ lemon*
*1 egg, beaten*
*little milk*

1 Lightly grease 2 baking sheets. Put the flours, salt, mixed spice and nutmeg in a bowl. Rub in the margarine until the mixture resembles fine breadcrumbs. Stir in the sugar, fruit and lemon rind. Make a well in the centre and gradually add the egg and enough milk to make a moist, stiff dough.

2 Spoon the mixture into small heaps on to the prepared baking sheets. Bake at 200°C (400°F) mark 6 for about 20 minutes or until golden brown. Transfer to a wire rack and leave to cool.

**Packing and storage** Wrap in plastic wrap or a paper napkin for transporting. Store in an airtight container for up to 3 days, or wrap and freeze.

## RASPBERRY BUNS

• Makes 16 •

100 g (4 oz) self-raising wholemeal flour
100 g (4 oz) self-raising white flour
salt
100 g (4 oz) polyunsaturated margarine
75 g (3 oz) soft light brown sugar
I egg
little milk
reduced sugar raspberry jam, to fill
milk, to glaze

I  Lightly grease 2 baking sheets. Put the flours and salt in a bowl. Rub in the margarine until the mixture resembles fine breadcrumbs. Stir in the sugar. Make a well in the centre and gradually add the egg and enough milk to make a stiff dough.

2  Turn out the dough on to a lightly floured surface and form into a roll. Cut off pieces 2 cm (¾ inch) thick and place on the prepared baking sheets. Make a hollow in the centre of each and fill with jam. Brush the buns with milk.

3  Bake at 200°C (400°F) mark 6 for 15–20 minutes or until golden brown. Transfer to a wire rack and leave to cool.

**Packing and storage** Wrap in plastic wrap or foil for transporting. Store in an airtight container for up to 3 days, or wrap and freeze.

## CHOCOLATE PEANUT BUTTERFLIES

• Makes 16 •

40 g (1½ oz) self-raising wholemeal flour
40 g (1½ oz) self-raising white flour
2.5 ml (½ level tsp) baking powder
25 g (1 oz) cocoa powder
100 g (4 oz) polyunsaturated margarine
75 g (3 oz) soft light brown sugar
2 eggs, beaten

**For the peanut topping**
45 ml (3 tbsp) low fat soft cheese, curd cheese
   or cottage cheese, sieved
45 ml (3 tbsp) smooth peanut butter
15 ml (1 tbsp) milk
10 ml (2 tsp) runny honey

I  Place sixteen paper cases in patty tins and set aside. Put the flours, baking powder and cocoa into a bowl and mix together. Add the margarine, sugar and eggs. Beat until smooth.

2  Divide the mixture between the paper cases. Bake at 200°C (400°F) mark 6 for 20–25 minutes or until well risen and firm. Leave to cool.

3  To make the topping, mix the cheese, peanut butter, milk and honey together until smooth.

4  Cut a slice from the top of each cake and cut in half. Spoon the topping on to the cakes and replace the halved cake slices on top at an angle to form butterfly wings.

**Packing and storage** Carefully wrap in plastic wrap or foil for transporting. Store in an airtight container for up to 2–3 days, or wrap and freeze at the end of step 2.

## PEANUT MUFFINS

• Makes 12 •

100 g (4 oz) plain white flour
100 g (4 oz) plain wholemeal flour
20 ml (4 level tsp) baking powder
15 ml (1 level tbsp) soft light brown sugar or
   runny honey
large pinch of salt
I egg
45 ml (3 tbsp) crunchy peanut butter
225 ml (8 fl oz) milk
50 ml (2 fl oz) oil

I  Put twelve paper cake cases into twelve deep muffin tins. Put the flours, baking powder, sugar and salt into a bowl and mix well.

2  Lightly beat the egg and stir in the peanut butter, milk and oil. Add the liquid to the dry ingredients and stir lightly until the flour is just moistened. Do not overbeat.

3  Spoon the mixture into the cake cases. Bake at 200°C (400°F) mark 6 for 20–25 minutes or until well risen and a fine skewer inserted into the centre comes out clean. Transfer to a wire rack and leave to cool.

**Packing and storage** Split and spread with a little polyunsaturated margarine. Wrap in plastic wrap for transporting. Store in an airtight container for up to 2 days, or wrap and freeze.

# CHERRY REFRIGERATOR BISCUITS

• Makes about 50 •

*100 g (4 oz) plain white flour*
*100 g (4 oz) plain wholemeal flour*
*5 ml (1 level tsp) baking powder*
*100 g (4 oz) polyunsaturated margarine*
*175 g (6 oz) soft light brown sugar*
*50 g (2 oz) glacé cherries, very finely chopped*
*5 ml (1 tsp) vanilla flavouring*
*1 egg, beaten*

1  Grease a baking sheet. Put the flours and baking powder into a bowl. Rub in the margarine until the mixture resembles fine breadcrumbs. Stir in the sugar, cherries and vanilla flavouring. Add the egg and mix to a smooth dough with a wooden spoon.

2  Turn out the dough on to a large sheet of foil and shape into a long roll about 5 cm (2 inches) in diameter. Wrap in the foil and chill in the refrigerator overnight.

3  Very thinly slice the roll into as many biscuits as required. The remainder of the roll can be wrapped again in the foil and returned to the refrigerator for up to 1 week.

4  Place the biscuits well apart on the prepared baking sheet. Bake at 190°C (375°F) mark 5 for 10–12 minutes or until golden. Cool on the baking sheet for a few minutes then transfer to a wire rack and leave to cool completely.

**Packing and storage**  Wrap in plastic wrap, foil or a plastic bag for transporting. Store in an airtight container for up to 2–3 days.

# GRANDMA'S BISCUITS

• Makes about 20 •

*50 g (2 oz) polyunsaturated margarine*
*75 g (3 oz) soft light brown sugar*
*15 ml (1 tbsp) golden syrup*
*50 g (2 oz) self-raising white flour*
*25 g (1 oz) self-raising wholemeal flour*
*1.25 ml ($\frac{1}{4}$ level tsp) bicarbonate of soda*
*50 g (2 oz) rolled oats*
*50 g (2 oz) American peanuts, finely chopped*
*25 g (1 oz) desiccated coconut*
*1 egg, beaten*

1  Lightly grease 2 baking sheets. Put the margarine, sugar and golden syrup in a heavy-based saucepan and heat gently until melted, stirring occasionally.

2  Put the flours, bicarbonate of soda, oats, peanuts and coconut in a large bowl and stir well to combine. Pour the melted mixture on to the dry ingredients with the beaten egg and stir well to mix.

3  Shape the mixture into about twenty small walnut-sized balls. Place the balls slightly apart on the prepared baking sheets. Flatten down with the back of a fork. Bake at 180°C (350°F) mark 4 for 12–15 minutes or until lightly browned. Cool on the baking sheets for a few minutes, then transfer to a wire rack and leave to cool completely.

**Packing and storage**  Wrap in plastic wrap, foil or a paper napkin for transporting. Store in an airtight container for up to 2 weeks.

# OATY FRUIT FLAPJACKS

• Makes 16 •

*50 g (2 oz) polyunsaturated margarine*
*50 g (2 oz) soft light brown sugar*
*45 ml (3 tbsp) golden syrup*
*100 g (4 oz) rolled oats*
*50 g (2 oz) sultanas*

1  Grease an 18 cm (7 inch) square cake tin. Put the margarine, sugar and syrup in a saucepan and heat gently, stirring until melted. Add the rolled oats and sultanas and mix well.

2  Turn the mixture into the prepared tin and press down well. Bake at 180°C (350°F) mark 4 for 20–25 minutes or until golden brown.

3  Allow to cool slightly in the tin, then mark into sixteen fingers with a sharp knife. When firm, cut right through. Leave to cool completely in the tin before removing.

**Packing and storage**  Wrap in plastic wrap or foil for transporting. Store in an airtight container for up to 2 weeks.

## LEMON AND NUT SHORTBREAD

• Makes about 16 •

50 g (2 oz) plain wholemeal flour
75 g (3 oz) plain white flour
100 g (4 oz) polyunsaturated margarine
50 g (2 oz) American honey roast peanuts,
    finely chopped
50 g (2 oz) soft light brown sugar
finely grated rind of 1 large lemon

1  Put the flours into a bowl. Rub in the margarine until the mixture resembles fine breadcrumbs. Stir in the peanuts, sugar and lemon rind.

2  Knead the mixture to form a smooth dough. Divide in half.

3  Roll out each piece of dough on a lightly floured surface to an 18 cm (7 inch) round and place on a baking sheet. Mark each round into 8 portions and prick all over with a fork. Crimp the edges to decorate.

4  Bake at 150°C (300°F) mark 2 for 35–45 minutes or until lightly golden brown. Leave to cool on the baking sheet. Cut in portions.

**Packing and storage**  Wrap in plastic wrap, a paper napkin or foil for transporting. Store in an airtight container for up to 3 days, or wrap and freeze.

# SWEET TREATS

## TRUFFLES

• Makes about 12 •

50 g (2 oz) plain, milk or white chocolate
25 g (1 oz) polyunsaturated margarine
50 g (2 oz) sponge cake, crumbled
25 g (1 oz) icing sugar, sifted
10 ml (2 tsp) orange, apple or pineapple juice
chocolate vermicelli, to coat (optional)

1  Break the chocolate into squares and place in a small heatproof bowl with the margarine. Stand the bowl over a saucepan of simmering water and stir until the chocolate has melted.

2  Stir in the cake crumbs, icing sugar and fruit juice. Cover and chill in the refrigerator for about 30 minutes or until the mixture is firm enough to handle.

3  Dust your fingers with icing sugar and divide the mixture into twelve and roll into small balls. Coat in the vermicelli, if using.

4  Put the truffles in petit four cases. Chill in the refrigerator until ready for transporting.

**Packing and storage**  Wrap in plastic wrap or foil for transporting. Store in the refrigerator for up to 2–3 weeks.

## CHOCOLATE DIPPED FRUITS

• Serves 4 •

100 g (4 oz) plain, milk or white chocolate
about 450 g (1 lb) firm fresh fruit such as
    strawberries, chunks of pineapple, grapes,
    orange segments

1  Break the chocolate into squares and place in a small heatproof bowl. Stand the bowl over a saucepan of simmering water and stir until the chocolate has melted.

2  Dip each piece of fruit in the chocolate so that it is half coated. Transfer the dipped fruits to a baking sheet and leave until the chocolate has set. Store in the refrigerator until ready for transporting.

**Packing and storage**  Wrap in plastic wrap or place in small lidded containers for transporting. Store in the refrigerator for up to 2 days.

# INDEX